AF560633

THEMES AND TECHNIQUES IN THE PLAYS OF EDWARD ALBEE

THEMES AND TECHNIQUES IN THE PLAYS OF EDWARD ALBEE

By

Dr. K. Suneetha Reddy

M.A (Eng.), M.Sc (Psy.), M.Phil, Ph.D.
Associate Professor & Head of the Dept.
S & H, Andhra Loyola Institute of
Engineering & Technology
Vijayawada (A.P.)
(India)

DISCOVERY PUBLISHING HOUSE PVT. LTD.
NEW DELHI-110 002

Published by:
Tilak Wasan

DISCOVERY PUBLISHING HOUSE PVT. LTD.
4383/4B, Ansari Road, Darya Ganj
New Delhi-110 002 (India)
Phone : +91-11-23279245, 43596064-65
Fax : +91-11-23253475
E-mail : discoverypublishinghouse@gmail.com
sales@discoverypublishinggroup.com
parul.wasan@gmail.com
web : www.discoverypublishinggroup.com

***First Edition:* 2014**

ISBN: 978-93-5056-513-1

Themes and Techniques in the Plays of Edward Albee

Printed at:
Dynamic Printers
Delhi

THE LIVING LEGEND

This Book is Dedicated
To
My Parents
My Husband
And
My Kids Pradyumna & Pranava

Preface

The book, *Themes and Techniques in the Plays of Edward Albee*, is the outcome of my research in the Department of English, Sri Venkateswara University, Tirupati. The present thesis unravels the mystery of Edward Albee - the playwright, through an assessment of his plays from their thematic view point, relating to the techniques used by Albee. Little did I know how true John Dryden's remarks are that 'It's hard to judge uprightly of the living', would prove true during the course of my research on Edward Albee.

It is only after I began my exploration of Edward Albee, did I come to realize that he is not that easy to assess as imagined. A living author is continually evolving and cannot be pinned down to a context as an author of the past can. Moreover Albee is a multilayered personality, where each layer unfolds a different quality, a different dimension; to be studied deeply. At some moments, I felt myself identifying with him, at other times I found him mysterious, detached and difficult to comprehend. Always on the look out for fresh interviews by the author, new works written by him, I spent many anxious moments trying to cope up with the latest material available. Since it is not possible to make a thorough study of all the plays of Edward Albee in this thesis, it is felt that it is better to restrict the study to a few prominent plays, since the same themes have been further explored by the dramatist in his other plays also.

The present thesis has been divided into seven chapters for the convenience of analysis. The subtitles for the chapters are the titles of Edward Albee's plays which add meaning to the subject discussed in the chapter.

The first chapter titled, Edward Albee: *The American Dream* introduces Albee as the new American dream. His biographical, social and literary influences are studied as they have formed major themes in most of his plays. It also traces his career as a dramatist; with his contribution to American literature and the situations at the time of his entry.

In the Second Chapter an attempt has been made to shed light on the origin, growth, and study about the pioneers of the absurd drama titled Absurd Drama - *Counting the Ways.* Six Plays - The Zoo Story, The Death of Bessie Smith, The Sandbox, The American Dream, Seascape and The Man Who had three Arms, have been selected to study Edward Albee as an Absurd dramatist.

In the third chapter titled Human Relationships - *A Delicate Balance,* the fundamental unit of the human community-family is presented. For Albee, human relationship is not only the first and foremost basic requirement for man, but also is the very indispensable principle that mankind should adopt, lest its survival be dubious. Relationships which are in a delicate balance within the family and outside, are studied in his plays, Who's Afraid of Virginia Woolf?, A Delicate Balance, All Over, Counting The Ways, The Lady From Dubuque and Finding The Sun.

Albee identifies 'illusion' to be an eclipsing factor in the life of man, which is dealt in the fourth chapter titled 'Illusion and Reality–*Who's Afraid of Virginia Woolf*? Illusion allures mankind, appears as affording comfort, entices man to evil path, and engulfs him in a hell upon earth which is best seen in Albee's The American Dream, Who's Afraid of Virginia Woolf?, Tiny Alice, Three Tall Women and The Play About the Baby.

Another major theme of Albee is alienation which is presented in the fifth chapter Alienation – *Finding the Sun.*

Albee illustrates by expounding how alienation, loneliness and rejection pose a great threat to the existence of the good human relationship. Four of Albee's plays The Zoo Story, The Death of Bessie Smith, Who's Afraid of Virginia Woolf? – and Tiny Alice are selected for the study.

In the sixth chapter titled Techniques – *The Man Who had Three Arms* an attempt has been made to discuss various techniques used in the plays of Edward Albee. Albee experiments with varying dramatic styles and playwriting techniques which has been studied in detail in most of his major plays. He is definitely a man with three arms are may be more.

The last and seventh chapter titled Summing Up – *All Over* sums up Edward Albee's literary talents which has earned him a permanent name in the history of literature. The subtitle 'All Over' doesn't mean that Albee's literary career is all over, but it means that his fame as a legendary dramatist has spread 'All Over'.

I am deeply indebted to my research supervisor Prof. G.M. Sundaravalli whose faith in me, made me have no choice but to live up to her expectations. She has not only provided with able guidance and wise counsel throughout the period of the study, but also has been a source of inspiration and encouragement. Her patience, attention and affection enriched me in matters of the subject, research outlook and the other associated areas. I am deeply beholden to her, and so, if it is not an exaggeration, my words are inadequate and these pages are insufficient to pen my indebtedness to my mentor, Prof. G.M. Sundaravalli.

I am indebted to all the faculty members of the Department of English, Sri Venkateswara University, Tirupati for giving me useful advices needed, from time to time. I am thankful to Mr. Hema Sekhar, Jr. Asst., Department of English, for his help in the process of my research work.

I am deeply indebted to my beloved parents Sri K. Sreeramulu Reddy and Smt. Sarojamma for their blessings and co-operation during the course of this study, without whose help it would have been a tough task for me to cope with my educational career. I owe myself to them.

I will be failing in my responsibility if I do not acknowledge my heart felt gratitude and thanks to my husband, Sri C.V.N. Reddy, who always stood by me as a great source of inspiration despite his busy schedules. My special appreciation goes to my children C. Pradyumna and C. Pranava and to my brother K. Hari Prasad Reddy for their co-operation and support in helping me to complete my research.

I am thankful to Ms Usha Sharma, for her cooperation in going through this dissertation and for making corrections.

I wish to record my thanks to all my friends who stood by me in my busy schedule for their cooperation in completing this work.

I thank the Director and the staff of the American Research Library, Hyderabad and SCHILET, Madurai for having provided me with material for reference during the course of my work.

–K. Suneetha

Acknowledgements

I am deeply indebted to my research supervisor Prof. G.M.Sundaravalli whose faith in me, made me have no choice but to live up to her expectations. She has not only provided with able guidance and wise counsel throughout the period of the study, but also has been a source of inspiration and encouragement. Her patience, attention and affection enriched me in matters of the subject, research outlook and the other associated areas. I am deeply beholden to her, and so, if it is not an exaggeration, my words are inadequate and these pages are insufficient to pen my indebtedness to my mentor, Prof. G.M. Sundaravalli.

I remain extremely thankful to all the faculty members of the Department of English, Sri Venkateswara University, Tirupati for giving me useful advices needed, from time to time.

I am deeply indebted to my beloved parents Sri K.Sreeramulu Reddy and Smt. Sarojamma for their blessings and co-operation during the course of this study, without whose help it would have been a tough task for me to cope with my educational career. I owe myself to them.

I will be failing in my responsibility if I do not acknowledge my heartfelt gratitude and thanks to my husband, Sri C.V.N. Reddy whc always stood by me as a great source of inspiration despite his busy schedule. My special appreciation goes to my children C. Pradyumna and C. Pranava and to my brother

K. Hari Prasad Reddy for their co-operation and support in helping me to complete my research.

I thank the Director and the staff of the American Research Library, Hyderabad and SCHILET, Madurai for having provided me with material for reference during the course of my work.

–K. Suneetha

Contents

1

Edward Albee
The American Dream

If Edward Albee had not existed, he would most certainly have been invented.[1]

The most polemical and 'the most talked about' playwright in the post-war era "Edward Albee came fully fledged as a playwright of international stature."[2] His enviable position in the dramatic world has remained unchanged ever since he burst onto the America's theatrical scene in the late 1950's, when Eisenhower years gave way to the Kennedy era. The prominent playwrights disappeared from the scene: political persecutions and public conservatism paralyzed Miller, personal problems immersed Tennessee Williams into oblivion, and O'Neill was dead. These seemed to favor the new playwright, Albee.

As Bigsby says, "America needed a new playwright but the economics of Broadway were such that the financial risks were too great to take a chance on untried talent".[3] When Albee entered the theatrical world, people were dissatisfied with the institution of the theatre, the form of the theatre, the boundaries of the theatre and the very nature of theatre. The institution was Broadway which was a 'symptom of dissatisfaction'. They were not prepared to introduce anything new and the very word 'experiment' was anathema to them. Naturally people expected that some young 'American' might perform miracles to redeem the theatre world from the abyss. And Albee, took the American theatre by storm, never disappointed his countrymen all through his dramatic career.

Of the three socially conscious playwrights, who rose to the occasion, only Albee survived. The other two Jack Gelber and Jack Richardson failed because of presenting 'fashionable European influence in the realist play', but Albee set his roots so firmly and spread his shoots so widely with his theater technique in a short span of time that no one could shake him.

Albee must be credited with the reinventing of the American stage at a time when its originality and quality seemed to be fading. He revitalized the American theatre by introducing European dramatic influences in a uniquely American context. In fact, he uses the themes of all absurd playwrights of Europe to portray the human condition, viz. isolation, alienation and loneliness, truth and illusion in an American way with an exclusive American idiom. Albee's plays startled the critics and the audiences with their intensity, their modern themes, and their experiments in form, while changing the landscape of American drama. He was unanimously hailed as the successor to Arthur Miller, Tennessee Williams, and Eugene O'Neill.

Albee's plays which are around 25 form a body work that is recognized as unique, uncompromising, controversial, elliptical and provocative. Albee himself describes it as "an examination of the American scene, an attack on the substitution for real values in our society, a condemnation of complacency, cruelty, and emasculation and vacuity, a stand against the fiction that everything in this slipping land of ours is peachy keen".[4] His forty-year career has seen as many commercial failures as well as successes. Albee feels that "There is not always a great relationship between popularity and excellence, you must have to make the assumption you're doing good work and go on doing it."[5] and the result is his non-stop experimental plays.

Albee's somewhat paradoxical position in American culture was perhaps summed up by the Kennedy Center's honors ceremony of 1996, at which he was lauded by the then President Clinton: "Tonight our nation … born in rebellion … pays tribute to you, Edward Albee in your rebellion … the American theatre was reborn"[6] Today he is frequently listed alongside Eugene O'Neill, Tennessee Williams and Arthur Miller as one of the nations great dramatists of the twentieth century. In a fragmented, post modern theatre culture full of young pretenders and competing multicultural voices, Edward Albee himself was a controversial young writer. Throughout his long career, who consistently refused to do what was expected of him –and so has to face applauds and brickbats.

The life of Edward Albee reads like a Horatio Alger story. "In the late nineteenth century the Alger heroes of "*Ragged Dick, Tattered Tom, Luck and Pluck, and Sink or Swim*"-all poor boys – inevitable rose to fame and wealth after struggling with temptation and poverty. All these young heroes brilliantly exemplified the idea that virtue always receives an ultimate reward –preferably in cold cash."[7] In the twentieth century, of course, everything is changed, and so have an alteration in the saga of 'the lucky orphan'. Albee has termed the history of his earliest years as a fascinating and wonderfully ironic tale of a rich boy who rose from riches to riches in a single generation.

Edward Albee was born on March 12, 1928 to a woman called Louise Harvey, whom he has not tried to trace. Though his natural parents abandoned him in infancy, he was adopted by a multi-millionaire, Reed Albee, and his wife Frances Albee of New York, within an age of two weeks, thus thrown into a home of enervating plenty. Nevertheless he ought to have enjoyed a golden childhood for he lived in a luxurious Tudor mansion. But it was not spared from being painful, owing to the fact that he was anxious, unstable, undisciplined, mediocre in studies, and truant, mainly because of a complete absence of want in all aspects of material luxury. Many critics suggest that the tense family conflicts of Albee's dramas are derived from his childhood experiences.

Edward Albee's resentment towards his natural parents was quite strong. He could not bring himself to forgive them for mercilessly discarding him and making him feel unwanted. This is quite apparent in the contempt with which he treats the family unit in virtually all his plays. As Debauccher points out, "the themes of the abandoned and adopted infant and magnificent but solitary vagabond are treated in the six of his first nine plays".[8] Albee's childhood experiences at home and in school resulted in his deep set of anger against the world in general and women in particular. The basis for many a portrait of domineering, aggressive and threatening women where he releases his pent of anger at his mother and of the effete and cowed men in his plays has been his own foster parents. His mother was twenty-three years younger and a foot taller than her husband, was extremely vocal, on the contrary, always ready to express her opinions in ringing tones of approbation or denunciation. Reed Albee, even though a leading millionaire in U.S.A, was a small silent man, eager to please his second wife and had fallen into a habit of continual agreement with anything she said or did in order to avoid argument. A picture of his foster parents, a domineering mother and a submissive father, can be observed in Mommy and Daddy of The American Dream and The Sandbox.

The only person whom Albee loved and felt comfortable was Mrs. Albee's mother. He dedicated his short play The Sandbox to her on her death bed in 1960. He says" I could communicate with her … she was at the end of it and I was at the beginning so both of us were outside the ring"[9] He presents Grandma Cotta as private humanity generating public harmony, contrasting it with that of his parents as a world of order and grace destroyed by human imperfection. Albee is of the conviction that Grandma Cotta stands at the verge of destruction of such perfection, and he at the end of such imperfection. By this Albee presents himself as an optimist of a perfect world. "We are nowhere near utopia anywhere on this planet but I do believe in the perfectibility of society. So I'm an optimist".[10]

Thus, being a liberal individualist innately, he could not contain himself to a stereo-type pattern of education that focused generally upon shaping students to a mass order. He was a bad school boy, and later a mediocre student, changed high schools three times, and ran away from the Military Academy at Valley Forge from where he was expected to learn discipline. Albee's education was chaotic, like Julia in A Delicate Balance (1966) failing to distinguish himself and becoming increasingly difficult. He finally obtained a diploma from the Choate School where he attempted to write poems and novels, but all in vain except one or two which he got published in the local magazines. He worked sincerely; sometimes wrote up to eighteen hours a day. He started his literary career by writing poems, short-stories, short plays and novels. Albee's first literary efforts were largely confined to poetry and he continued to think of himself primarily as a poet until well into his twenties but he was not successful as expected and he could not get due recognition from the audience.

Thus began Albee's ten year struggle for existence. These years have been called his 'bohemian era' but Albee calls them his 'peddling years'. After leaving home he moved to New York's Greenwich Village. To earn his livelihood, the adolescent vagabond 'worked in a series of menial jobs'. Jerry Tallmer describes this period as "an era the very odor of which permeates the life and lines of Jerry the lonely psychotic in The Zoo Story."[11] The seed to become a playwright for Edward Albee was sown during this period. His outlook towards life was considerably influenced by his odd jobs. He wanted time to write, but also to absorb everything around him.

Albee met William Flanagan-the composer and musicologist who became his lover and his most important, most perceptive mentor with whom he was to spend the next nine years of his life. Friendship with him proved useful for Albee as he was introduced to and brought in contact with famous personalities in the literary and music worlds. With music Albee developed an everlasting relationship as he himself says "I have an extraordinary relationship with music ... I go into a sort of training before I write a play."[12] Albee achieved limited success as an author of poetry and fiction before turning to drama.

On his thirtieth birthday, Albee started his career as a dramatist by writing a short play about an encounter between two strangers in Central Park, a terrible, moving vision of urban loneliness-The Zoo Story. It received its first performance in Berlin in 1959 on a double bill with *Krapp's Last Tape* after being rejected by New York producers who, though interested, considered it too explosive and too experimental. But when the play did open at Provincetown playhouse in 1960, it was so highly acclaimed by critic and the public alike that it established the young playwright in his native land. Edward Albee had found a way at last. There was no looking back now. With hopes of the public pinned upon him he decided to take up playwriting as a career. He had now achieved a sizeable inheritance and with the worry of finance off his mind he could devote full time to writing plays.

The impact of The Zoo Story was reinforced by the performance of The Death of Bessie Smith - 1960 (another Berlin premier) and The Sandbox, commissioned by the Spoleto Festival, both performed in the same year in New York. Albee's The American Dream, a play which has the characters of The Sand Box has been performed in 1961 and a full length play for which he had two titles in his mind: The Exorcism, or Who's Afraid of Virginia Woolf? was rapidly completed and performed in 1962. Who's Afraid of Virginia

Woolf? produced on Broadway in 1961 won him number of awards but, short of the Pulitzer Prize. In four years of writing and two years of his New York debut, Albee had emerged as a dramatist second to none in United States. His works were beginning to appear in print, and his first full-length play Who's Afraid of Virginia Woolf, was a smash hit in Broadway.

"Careers are mysterious things"[13] Albee ruminated at the time, when his first plays were received. Albee continued to experiment with a variety of forms, subjects and styles in his succeeding plays. In his works there was a power of imagination, versatility and a sheer talent comparable with many critics with the pioneering genius of American Theatre, Eugene O'Neill. The effect of premature fame on a young dramatist might well prove very damaging to his creative growth. More than one news writer said as much in print on the occasion of Albee's being 'luttered over by the reviewers'- even before the tumultuous success of Virginia Woolf.

All these factors definitely point towards one important aspect. Personal experience is intrinsically built through the trope of the child in the world of Albee's plots and characters. Albee's personal life, his childhood, his experiences in the society, his association with friends did affect his writing, no matter how vehemently Albee tried to segregate his childhood and adolescent experiences from his works, the influences undeniably existed. The love and bondage between a parent and a child could not be seen in his plays because he never enjoyed it.

There are frequent suggestions of themes which are very personal obsessions in the dramatist. The fondling child appears in play after play. Jerry in The Zoo Story, who tries desperately to make human contact, is abandoned, and has in his room an empty picture frame but no photograph of his lost parents. The adopted child in The American Dream is treated as an unsatisfactory piece of merchandise and as a consequence is progressively mutilated to diminish its ability to annoy Mommy and Daddy. "That's the way things are today:

you just can't get satisfaction, you just try."[14] In one form or another loss of the child or parent is behind Albee's play from fantasy child in Who's Afraid of Virginia Woolf? to the substitute-mother Elizabeth in The Lady from Dubuque. The other play that has been considered until now to be explicitly autobiographical is Three Tall Women which was 'conceived' as an act of reconciliation with his adoptive mother Frances (Frankie) Albee. In his introduction to the Three Tall Women, Albee confessed that it took him all his life to write the play where he emphasized –the schizophrenic ability and of writing both –the lived and living.

Albee stressed on the theme of alienation in almost all his plays which reveals his experiences in his childhood where he never enjoyed companionship, love or affection of his parents. He led a solitary life and he was alienated in every aspect which was expressed in his plays. Frustration, loneliness, alienation, lack of communication, lack of love in his relationship with his adoptive mother-and also with his biological mother-became converted into textual form in many of his dramas. Albee's shattering personal experiences and perilous upbringing taught this rebellious restless spirit of America to look at life like a lost soul seeking faith. Throughout his mature life Albee remains a searcher.

He prefers the public to judge a work for itself rather than search the author in it as he feels that "no worth-while piece of literature is any good if it has to be related to some biographical factor in the author's life."[15] Edward Albee claims that there is very little in his life of 'such great apparent significance or of earth shaking importance that would lead to this or that play.' This statement clearly indicated that Edward Albee, the introvert, hates the very idea of exposing himself to the public. He would like to retain his reputation as Flanagan refers to Albee as a 'chronically ambivalent man' and a 'widely reputed mysterious number.' This ambivalence can be found in his works also where he refrains from giving a definite solution to any problem.

Every writer whether a poet, novelist or a dramatist is subject to various influences of which literary influences is an important one which shapes and moulds the writer. Apart from biographical influences Edward Albee has been influenced by many writers, as Albee himself remarked, "I've been influenced by everybody, for God's sake. Everything I've seen, either accepting or rejecting it."[16] Critics have identified numerous and diverse influences from Unamuno to Strindberg to The Tatler to Tennessee Williams to medieval moralities to Vaudeville to Piano Pieves by Satie to humorous sketches by Thornton Wilder. He mainly used the savage ironical world of Samuel Beckett and Eugene Ionesco as his subject matter in almost all his plays. Albee placed his faith in the 'absolute need for an opening on to the intimate reality of others.'

The influences on Albee are foreign particularly those of French avant-garde for which Albee professes a strong attachment. "Albee has absorbed from the French Playwrights all there is to absorb-the Ionesco like fragmentation of a language no longer functional, the Beckett-like economy of plot, the symbolic suggestions of Adamov, the raw exposures of Genet, the sensitive portraits of Giraudoux."[17]

Albee followed some of the playwrights like Eugene Ionesco, Samuel Beckett and Jean Genet. He along with the American playwrights has succeeded in assimilating rather than copying their techniques and in molding these techniques in such a way that his work emerges as both integral and original in itself. Albee was able to excel some of his contemporary playwrights and he was successful in the use of language and in replacing Eugene Ionesco clichés and 'artificial assimil language'. As Martin Esslin says, "The language of The American Dream resembles that of Ionesco in its masterly combination of clichés. But these clichés, in their euphemistic, baby talk tone, are as characteristically American as Ionesco is French. The most disagreeable varieties are hidden behind the corn-fed cheeriness of advertising jingles and family magazine unctuousness."[18]

The Sandbox is the closest that Albee has ever come to produce as an absurd play in the European sense. There are clear indications that his personal vision stops short of Samuel Beckett's Nihilism. It is also seen that in The American Dream the divergence between Albee's and Beckett's particular visions become more immediately evident. It is said that The American Dream was a direct importation from an experimental European theatre. Gilbert Debaussher calls it, "Albee's frankest incursion into the theatre of the Absurd."[19] The idea of The American Dream itself had in fact provided the subject for Eugene O'Neill's Marco Millions, Clifford Odet's, *Awake and Sing*, Arthur Miller's *The Death of a Salesman* and Tennessee Williams, *Camino real.* Albee has also used means in describing the shallowness of the family and the disappearance of individualism in a mechanized society, themes which Ionesco continually developed from *The Bald Soprano* to *Rhinoceros.* A Delicate Balance is a classic study of American family life in the mode of O'Neill's *Long's Day's Journey into Night.* Albee used a good number of props and the symbolism which was present in Ionescan theatre. Even though Edward Albee has followed some of the techniques of Ionesco and Samuel Beckett, his plays are more accepted. The short plays of Samuel Beckett and Ionesco were failures but Edward Albee proved his real talent in this aspect.

Albee is quite categorical about the influences on him. He does not agree with the fact that he is very much influenced by the contemporary playwrights. As a playwright, he feels that he has been influenced by every single play he has ever experimented. According, to him, 'influences is a matter of selection of acceptance and rejection.' What he wants to impress upon critics is that when there is an influence of a particular author one should not jump to the conclusion that he has borrowed a particular author or imitated that particular author. He wants that people should know that 'similarities of people writing in the same generation, in the same century' are inevitable. What is important is that the borrowed idea and principle should be properly fused. What Albee has been attempting all through his works is an exploration of possibilities of ideas which may be found in others also. After all, the theatre of the Absurd also represents a group of dramatists who "seem to be doing something vaguely in similar ways at approximately the same time through out the continent"[20] to which Albee is no exception.

It is imperative that a writer be affected by the prevailing conditions of his age. Edward Albee is no different from this. In and around Albee's period the social, literary and intellectual climate activated the young and impressionable mind of the playwright. The early twentieth century was an age in which the need for the change in the mode of writing in every sphere was felt. An age as complex as the twentieth century could no longer be portrayed faithfully though the earlier dramatic conventions.

American Drama in the mid-century and afterwards reflected the resultant changes in the people's outlook behavior and the patterns of society due to the devastating effects of the Second World War. The Americans were self-reliant individuals, filled with patriotic spirit, after the war, were less sure and less hopeful of their future. The World's peace was threatened and it affected the individuals in families in America too and that in an insidious way. The American society and the family unit encountered profound changes; the family values tended to change and the society moved towards material and commercial advancement. Dollars and cents usurped the position of love and affection in the family and in society. Commercialism, lack of love, and loss in values in the family land, the failure and difficulty of human communication symbolized the absurdity of existence. The post-war generation, which escaped the depression through the skin of its teeth, was left with disillusionment and a sense of loss of the past and an awareness of the emptiness of the present. Despite the economic freedom, the age, as the aged Father in Micheal V Gazzo's *A Hatful of Rain* remarks, "is the age of the vacuum. The people-they don't believe any more."[21] A grim mood prevailed; people were troubled by the depressing and insecure life of the period. They attempted to adjust themselves to the external world, which could hardly be comprehended. Hence, the American individuals, being alienated and baffled, struggled to maintain both identity and dignity.

America, after mid-century turned out to be a success oriented society. The word 'success' has a unique meaning peculiar to America. It is associated with material wealth and opulence. Success in life was equated to financial success. It is seldom referred to spiritual or metaphysical goals. The dichotomy between the actual and the popular, the truth and illusion, the ideal and practical is beautifully synthesized in European dramas by bringing a spiritual purgation with the illusion of love, power and dignity in life. But the American illusion of success-is totally materialistic. This is American contribution to the modern drama. The American, living in a highly technological civilized world which offers him an unlimited expectation of material welfare-a promise yet to be fulfilled for millions-looks depressed, harassed and alienated. He is anxious or avaricious to earn more money, success and social status devoid of grace, dignity and kindness, ready to stake or risk anything for it. Man's sense of value as Eric Fromm observes in *The Art of Living*, "depends upon his success: whether he can sell himself favorably ... If the individual fails in a profitable investment of himself, he feels that he is a failure, if he succeeds he is a success".[22]

The radical changes that came about in the society prompted the emergence of the Beat Movement, which protested against Man's condition in society. The works of Keronac, Ginsberg and other writers of the movement brought out the emptiness of conventional society. Following Ginsbag's "Howl" the Beats, in order to demonstrate their protest against conventional society, adopted unconventional ways in dress and living and also in their attitude toward life, which they have condemned as a "howl".

In the fifties, the absurd plays from abroad ... Genets *No Exit*, Ionesco's *Rhinoceros* and Becketts *Waiting for Godot* ... which attacked the loss of moral and spiritual values in an absurd, war-ridden world were received with interest. They greatly influenced the American stage of the fifties and after. American literature seems to cater to the needs of the people for a change occurred in almost every walk of life. The dissatisfaction seen in politics and society is found reflected in American Drama. The dissatisfaction seen in politics and society is found reflected in American drama by O'Neill-the only representative to feel the pulse of this and provide a remedy for it. By inclinations and circumstances, Eugene O'Neill concerns himself with the inner conflicts, a searching for meaning and order, an awareness of the controlling forces for the expression of these troubles. Eugene O'Neill applies expressionism in spite of realism which fails to probe deeper. In the qualities mentioned above there seems to be a sense of crawling for some experiment unknown in American theatre which in course of time takes the form of a characteristic quality of the drama of the 'absurd'. The sense of freedom that O'Neill stimulates is immediately found reflected in his plays.

Although American Drama at mid-century is a recognized force in the world of drama, it is unfortunately true that American dramatists with international reputation are only a handful. Describing the condition of American stage and that of the leading playwrights of the time Meserve says:

> Miller upholds the dignity of man, Williams denies it; one concerned himself with man's soul, the other with man's organs. One searches for meaning, the other assumes a vold and creates a sensation to compensate for man's sorrowful loss. One tries to find man in a real world the other sees man as a part of a romantic vision.[23]

After the fifties we enter the sixties, a period of great upheaval from different points of view. The Eisenhower administration saw the end of McCarthy era as well as the conclusion of fifties. John Kennedy's assassination cast a shadow over sixties. Lyden Johnson became the President and the Americans were in the Mire of the Vietnam War. But in spite of all these changes in the political life of America, American dissent had again grown strong and vocal-strong in the sense that it was not to be silenced easily. The 1960's seemed to be dedicated to a variety of adventures in the new theatre of the so called 'absurd'. This theatre is however, a significant expression of the frustration which has entered modern man's life due to various reasons-political, social and individual. This frustration is seen in the wailing and gnashing of teeth or subdued grief in the plays of the representative writers.

Frustration leads, finally, to revolt or sometimes to protest. This revolt or protest, whatever it is, got expressed in the drama of the 'absurd'. The 'absurd' drama has nothing to be either a weapon to use in class struggle or in the war against poverty or unemployment or for class or racial oppression which the drama of the Thirties had been. The 'absurd' drama rarely cares for the subtleties of characterization because the larger issues are at stake. The drama of the 'absurd', it must be said, presents an awareness of absurdity of life. It means that though absurdity was in extent already present, but it has recently come to the notice of the playwrights. The absurd drama which only raised questions without demanding answers, was congenial to the intellectual atmosphere of the sixties that was disturbed by the social unrest, revolt, and uncertainties raised by the developments in nuclear science and space research.

In the American society the conflict of opinion between old and young is seen in the differences of belief and attitude where the generation gap gapes. The disturbed world with social and political evils and devastating effects of the nuclear energy made the people of America lose faith in moral and social values. Dope addiction was found to be common among teen-agers and the last graders in schools. The younger generations' protest against the traditional ways of the society led to free exploitation of sex, nudity and vulgar and dirty words in both plays and films. This impact is found in most of the Albee's plays.

In a success oriented and money based society, material possessions were viewed as the standards of an ideal living; the people discarding the conventional values substituted them with artificial values, which resulted in the ruin of harmony in the family and society.

Albee, who appeared on the American theatre scene with his exciting contribution to the American theatre world found himself trapped in a 'demoralized nation that has been eroded by futile war, economic disaster, political corruptions, drugs, hatred and other evils' The ideals of American community as foreseen by them have been destroyed by the racial strife, decentralization of family, decline of human relationship, substitution of artificial for real values, inclination to isolate and withdraw oneself and the tendency to seek shelter in illusion. Albee's plays found expression of a sense of loss at the collapse of a model community, or a social vision that dominated the world in the past. Through the presentation of moral and social problems of his time, he aimed at making the audience confront the real situations and mediate on the possibility of remedies. Albee likes to think that his audiences are influenced by his plays and as a result of sharing the life experience with his characters they leave the theatre, changed. The purpose of writing for Albee is "to present the world and the people in it as he sees it and say 'Do you like it? If you don't like it change it".[24]

Since, Edward Albee laments the loss of cultural and moral values, he has been dubbed a pessimist and defeatist. The intensity of Albee's view of American society and his passionate attack on complacency did not prove congenial to all his first critics. He indicated a futile materialism in a witty and abrasive style which made the underlying feelings all the more convincing and disconcerting. He seemed to hold up a distorting mirror to society, showing its values to be incoherent and inhuman. With the appearance of The American Dream the playwright was anathematized as nihilist, immoral and defeatist. He was too clearly identifiable with the un-American complications of the new European writing for him not to be assigned immediately to the Theatre of Absurd. However, the bleakness of Albee's vision was not absurdism nor any species of philosophical nihilism, but the result of a commitment to values he saw neglected or ignored. He was as much an 'angry young man' of American theatre as an absurdist.

Albee, indeed, emerges as an cptimist, an ardent moralist who attacks the false values of human life in order to honor the real values that will enhance the dignity of man; the deeper the level of despair that is struck in his plays, the deeper is the hope implied in them. Like his Julian in Tiny Alice he has been dedicated to reality rather than to appearance. The responsibility of a playwright, for Albee is to present a true-to-life picture, to bring about amelioration. He attempts to shake the audience out of their complacency into a revelation. Against the criticism that he tears things down and never builds up, Albee justifies himself by saying, "you can't build on the previous structure, you can't build on rubble, you've got to build on level ground, you've got to raze something before you raise"[25]

Albee shocks his audience with his apocalyptic vision of the stark realities of the human existence. Albee being angry and indignant at the society grows impatient and satirizes relentlessly as Strindberg, Ibsen and Shaw. Since, Edward Albee is considered to be an absurd dramatist; his plays naturally deal with the themes of despair, frustration, suffocation, tyranny and cruelty of society. They reveal the pointlessness, the meaninglessness of life and the difficulty of communication. Edward Albee has pointed out and exposed various aspects of social evils existing in the American society during his time like alienation and lack of communication, fantasy and realism, loss of relationships between family members, racial discrimination between Whites and Negroes. Albee's main intention in revealing all these social evils is only to bring out social change and to better the moral standards of people. It is apt to quote in his own words from his preface to The American Dream, "The purpose of the play is, to offend-as well as amuse and entertain; and every honest work is a personal private yowl, a statement of an individual's pleasure and pain."[26]

In almost all his plays Edward Albee tells that the world being desperate and ugly, people also are desperate and ugly. Albee's view is that life has no content, life is nothing and one must have courage to face the emptiness without fear. His plays are mainly about people and their life. In the words of Diana Trilling, "Albee's plays are about people who cared very deeply about each other and who tried hard to be decent, people whose hopes were right for themselves and each other, but who here for reasons beyond their control because they truly reside in the human situation, had defeated their decency, their love and hope."[27] Edward Albee, considered as an outraged social critic, taking sides with the victimized and the oppressed, protested against social injustice. Michael E. Rutenberg says, "Albee turns his social microscope on the very essence of our civilization, revealing immorality, opportunism, cruelty, hypocrisy, and sterility in the private of those whose job it is to shape and guide the tastes and morals of this country's next generation."[28]

The human condition becomes the nerve centre of each of his plays. His vision is testimony to the ways by which men and women seek in bad faith, to avoid their responsibilities as human beings. Albee said in 1959, "My plays examine people who are not living their lives fully, dangerously, properly."[29] His plays are concerned with the plight of the man in the modern age. The major absurdist themes like "the failure of verbal communication; the falsity of apparent reality; the inability of human beings to discern meaning in the world or purpose in their lives; are present in his plays"[30] He attempts to portray these themes by portraying realistic characters striving to fit their lives into meaningful patterns.

What Edgar Allen Poe has wished of playwrights, Albee fulfils in his plays ... to create new forms and develop new techniques ... so that he could express the American way of life better. The influence of O'Neill and European writers has encouraged him to experiment in various dramatic techniques and adopt various forms from naturalism to symbolism, from expressionism to surrealism and from absurd to avant-garde.

Albee's career was characterized by a long apprenticeship of trail and error experimentation, followed by a sudden, almost meteoric rise to success and notoriety. He has shown a fascination for a wide variety of theatrical styles and subjects throughout his career. The Zoo Story, which received its American debut on a double bill with a play by Samuel Beckett and which was favorably compared with the elder playwright's work, conveyed the alienation and disillusionment of the existentialist drama. Drawing on the poverty of his own life at that time and on his own experience while working in 'the city of people, Albee later described the experience of writing the play as a kind of revelation for him; it was the first time he felt as if the characters' language and rhythms were simply flowing, unforced from his subconscious. The Zoo story also proved a revelation in the context of the American theatre of the time, embodying onstage the restless, youthful energy of the disenfranchised 'Beat' generation, as well as providing a homegrown response to the recent innovations of European 'absurdist' playwrights such as Samuel Beckett.

In 1960, Albee explored American race relations in the southern Gothic atmosphere of The Death of Bessie Smith. Albee continued to build his reputation as an innovator in the absurdist manner with such one-act plays as The Sandbox (1959) and The American Dream (1960). Mainstream success came with the production of Who's Afraid of Virginia Woolf? on Broadway in 1961, won him a number of awards. In the following year his next original play the unorthodox Tiny Alice (1964)-a metaphysical dream play in which Albee explores his persistent theme of reality versus illusion, this time out in mystical, abstract and even religious terms, became the talking point of the season. A Delicate Balance (1964) in the mode of O'Neills Long Day's Journey into Night shows classic studies of American family life. It was widely faulted by critics for lacking action and cohesive ideas, it nevertheless garnered approval for its synthesis of dramatic elements and was awarded the Pulitzer Prize. In January 1966, however, Albee's second novel adaptation, based on James Purdy's Malcolm, closed on Broadway inside a week, after receiving universally dismissive reviews, it was clear that the honeymoon was over. Over the next decade and a half, Albee's star went into decline with critics and public alike, as show after show closed on Broadway after runs that were modest at best. Part of the problem was that critics tended to compare every new play unfavorably to Who's Afraid of Virginia Woolf ?

Albee continued to experiment in his succeeding plays; and while several of them failed commercially and elicited scathing reviews for their abstract classicism and dialogue, many scholars have commended his commitment to theatrical experimentation and refusal to pander to commercial pleasures. Though, Albee was doing what he had always done, following his creative nose wherever it led-which was often into distinctly un-commercial territory, some of his works proved too formalistic or intellectually oriented to be popularly appealing. After a series of set backs, in, 1975 Albee won his second Pulitzer prize with Seascape, which combined theatrical experiment and social commentary in a story about the retired vacationing couple who meet a pair of sea lizards at the beach. This play was regarded by some as pretentious but was commended overall for its lyrical quality and insights into the human condition. Albee seems to have relished the chance to write unassuming 'chamber pieces' for more intimate spaces, just as he had with Listening and Counting the Ways –two companion one-acts that first appeared together in 1977 at the Hartford Stage company, in Connecticut.

Throughout the 1970s Albee also struggled with alcoholism, but through his "drying out" period toward the end of the decade, he seems to have facilitated a new burst of creativity with three new plays appearing in the four years at the start of the 1980s-the critical responses to his work proved more hostile than ever. The Lady from Dubuque (1980), Lolita (1981, adapted from Nabokov's novel), and The Man Who Had Three Arms (1983) were all assaulted with a ferocity out of all proportion to whatever crimes against taste or dramaturgy they might have committed. Albee, it seemed, was now yesterday's man, a remnant of the 1960s completely out of place in the new, Reaganite.

Although he suffered through a decade of plays that refused to yield a commercial hit in the 1980's, Albee experienced a stunning success with Three Tall Women (1994) which won him his third Pulitzer Prize as well as Best Play awards from the New York Drama Critics Circle and Outer Critics Circle. He had previously won Pulitzers for A Delicate Balance (1966) and Seascape (1975). Other awards include an Obie Award (1960) and a Tony Award (1964).

It was nearly two decades before another new Albee play was premiered on Broadway. The 1980s marked the beginning of Albee's a new phase, during which he had, in effect, to start again from scratch, gradually rebuilding a life and reputation for himself. Regarded as a failed has-been in the New York theatre world, Albee decided to go where he was wanted, and began accepting invitations from colleges and universities to speak, to teach, and to direct plays. He developed, for example, a longstanding relationship with the University of Houston, in Texas, where he still regularly teaches a spring-semester playwriting class–thus continuing his commitment to mentoring new writing talent. Yet Albee's own writing benefited, too, from this period in the theatrical "wilderness." Various new plays were written to commission for small low-profile theatres, including Finding the Sun (1983) for the University of Northern Colorado, Marriage Play (1987) for the English Theatre in

Vienna, Austria, and Fragments (1993) for the Ensemble Theatre of Cincinnati. At first glance, these relatively short pieces might also seem fairly insubstantial: indeed, Fragments is subtitled "A Sit-Around," in self-deprecating recognition of that fact that the characters simply sit around and talk, without apparent purpose or "thorough line." Yet closer examination of these plays reveals all kinds of intriguing undercurrents in mood and characterization, as well as some ingenious formal games with scene structures The Play about the Baby was received coolly by the viewers, and was regarded as one of Albee's most important plays in 2001. Released from the pressure of being a "major American playwright," writing "major plays" for Broadway, still sufficient to rebel and evolve as the first playwright to provide a sympathetic treatment of bestiality on the Broadway stage–with 2002's The Goat, or who is Sylvia? –Albee seems to delight, even now, in prodding and unsettling conventional sensibilities, often with a kind of vaudevillian glee. And yet he is also a deeply serious, highly erudite figure, very much a member of the literary establishment. He is in short, a writer with many faces, many moods.

Albee's latest play to appear in New York in 2002 The Occupant concerns the life of sculptor Louise Nevelson, played by Anne Bancroft. The playwright and Ms. Nevelson, who died in 1988, were friends, and their conversations and friendship form the narrative, which concerns her marriage and subsequent abandonment of her husband and child, as well as her creative years. Ms. Bancroft comments of the play: "It's about a woman fighting the traditions and conventions she was forced into, in order to find her own path in life."[31] When Edward Albee's one-act two-hander The Zoo Story shook up the New York theater scene in 1960, the character of Peter was a blank slate of a man, provoked to animalistic life by a stranger. The playwright revisits the character in his new work, Peter and Jerry, (2004) a one-act being presented alongside that seminal play. Albee has said in recent interview that he felt Peter needed to be explored in more depth than he had been in Zoo Story. He envisions Peter's life before he takes the fateful trip to the park, returning to one of his favorite subjects-marriage. The deft and engaging new play adds depth to a classic.

Albee's work has been a continuous theatrical experiment, exploring and expanding the boundaries of American drama. Albee resists any attempt to label or categorize his work, arguing that all his plays are realistic, although some may be more stylized than others: "I think every experience we have is both, real and a metaphor. I don't see why this shouldn't be true for art. Most writers write in the hope that the problems they write about will disappear one day. What I hope is that my plays will encourage people to participate in their lives more."[32] The outspoken playwright, teacher and social critic is known for his fierce integrity, continuing to write despite any negative response to his work.

In spite of being thematically similar, all his plays are marked by distinctive and diverse characteristics, the colors and contours of which set one play apart from the other. These features shall be highlighted in detailed analyses in the forthcoming chapters.

REFERENCES

1. C.W.E. Bigsby, *A Critical Introduction to Twentieth Century American Drama*, Vol. III, (New York: Cambridge University Press), p. 249.
2. Gerry McCarthy; *Edward Albee*, (Macmillan Publisher Ltd., 1987), p. 3.
3. C.W.E.Bigsby, *A Critical Introduction to Twentieth Century American Drama*, Vol. III, (New York: Cambridge University Press), p. 249.
4. Edward Albee: Preface, *The American Dream* Coward McCann, Inc. New York.
5. Article 'The John F. Kennedy Center, for the Performing Arts" Internet (online).
6. Stephen Bottoms, *Introduction: The Man who had Three lives* Internet (Online).

7. Richard E.Amacher: *Edward Albee* (Twayne Publishers, Inc. New York, 1969) p. 15.
8. Gilbert Debusscher: *Edward Albee: Tradition and Renewal* (Brussels American Studies Centre), p. 2.
9. Anon, *Albee: Odd Man in on Broadway*, Newsweek (February, 1963) p. 51.
10. C.W.E. Bigsby, *A Critical Introduction to Twentieth Century American Drama*, Vol. III, (New York: Cambridge University Press) p. 279.
11. Jerry Tallmer, *Edward Albee, Playwright* New York Post, Sunday Magazine Section (November 4, 1962) p. 10.
12. C.W.E. Bigsby, *A Critical Introduction to Twentieth Century American Drama*, Vol. III, (New York: Cambridge University Press) p. 270.
13. Gerrry McCarthy; *Edward Albee*, (Macmillan Publisher Ltd., 1987) p. 3.
14. Edward Albee: *The American Dream* Coward McCann, Inc. New York, p. 16.
15. Charles Krohn & Julian Wasserman, Interview (March 18, 1981) *Edward Albee: An Interview and Essays*, Julian Wasserman, ed. Lee Lecture Series (Texas: The University of St. Thomas, Houstan, 1983), p. 14.
16. *Talk with Author,* Newsweek, 29 October 1962, 52-53 Phillip C.Kolin and J Madison Davis – Critical Essays on Edward Albee – p. 7.
17. Anne Paolucci, *From Tension to Tonic: The Plays of Edward Albee*, (Carbondale, 1972), p. 5.
18. Martin Esslin, *Theatre of Absurd* (Doubleday, 1961), p. 302.
19. Gilbert Debusscher, *Edward Albee: Tradition and Renewal,* Trans, A.D.Williams, (Brussel 1967), p. 2.
20. *Albee, Which Theatre is the Absurd One?* p. 146 As Quoted in Richard E. Amacher, *Edward Albee*, (Twayne Publishers, Inc.: New York]
21. Micheal V Gazzo, *A Hatful of Rain*, Best American Plays, 4th Series– 1951-1957, ed. John Gassner (1958, rpt New York Crown Publishers, Inc., 1970), p. 183.
22. Eric Fromn, *The Art of Living* (London, 1957) Quoted in C.W.E. Bigsby "A Critical Introduction to Twentieth Century American Drama", (London: Cambridge University Press, 1984) p. 4.
23. J. Walter Meserve, *An Outline History of American Drama*, (New Jeresy: Toronto, 1970), p. 262.

24. Digby Diehl, *Edward Albee Interviewed*, Transatlantic Review No. 13 (Summer 1963), p. 72.
25. *Interlude*, Choate Literary Magazine, (May 1946), pp. 5-10.
26. Gilbert Debusscher, *Edward Albee: Tradition and Renewal* Trans; Anne D.Williams (Brussles, 1967), p. 8.
27. Diana Trilling, *The Riddle of Albee's Who's Afraid of Virginia Woolf ?* in Edward Albee: Twentieth Century Views – A Collection of Critical Essays, ed. By C.W.E. Bigsby 1975, p. 86.
28. Michael E. Rutenberg, *Edward Albee: Playwright in Protest*, (October 1970) p. 31.
29. Roudane C. Mathew, *Understanding Edward Albee*, Columbia: University of South Carolina Press, 1987, p. 193.
30. R.M Coe. *Beyond Absurdity: Albee's Awareness of Audience in Tiny Alice* – Modern Drama, Vol. 18, December 1975, p. 372.
31. Gerry McCarthy, *Introduction: Edward Albee* (London: Macmillan Publishers Ltd. 1987) p. 8.
32. The Playwrights Speak (New York: Delacorte Press 1967), p. 51.

2

Absurd Drama

Counting The Ways

From Harmony, from heavenly Harmony

This universal frame began ...[1]

... sang Dryden during the gay days of the Restoration. The modern writers, living in far more troubled times have, on the other hand, found this 'universal frame' out of all harmony ... in other words, literally 'absurd'. Hence the rise of the kind of the drama during the nineteen fifties which as Edward Albee puts it, dealt essentially with 'man's attempt to make sense for himself out of his senseless position in a world which makes no sense ... which makes no sense because the moral, religious, political and social structures man has erected to 'illusion' himself have collapsed'. Taking man's fate as absolute Sisyphusian toil, many writers who hailed from different countries wrote in different languages to express the existential anguish of the human condition. Since Edward Albee is considered an 'absurd' dramatist, it is not out of place in this chapter to discuss about the origin and growth, of absurd drama and Albee's contribution to absurd drama with particular reference to his plays.

The word 'absurd' is much used and abused in contemporary American Drama. According to Martin Esslin the word 'absurd' means "out of harmony with reason or propriety, incongruous, unreasonable, and illogical."[2] Eugene Ionesco in his essay to 'Kakfa' defines the term thus, "Absurd is that which is devoid of purpose ... cut off from his religious, metaphysical and transcendental roots, man is lost in all his action, becomes senseless, absurd, useless."[3]

The word 'absurd' in theatrical terms is defined in many ways. It is not a birth but a rebirth, not a discovery but a rediscovery, not a search but a research. Martin Esslin and other critics have analyzed its traditions and correlated it to the old traditions. Esslin lays emphasis on the nature of the 'absurd' and says that:

> It represents a return to the original, religious function of the theatre-confrontation of man with the spheres of myth and religious reality. Like ancient Greek tragedy ... Theatre of the Absurd is intent in making its audience aware of man's precarious and mysterious position in the Universe.[4]

The 'absurd' is not a system but a philosophy on stage. It is a philosophical vision of cosmic, social and psychological disorder. According to Martin Esslin the writers of the Absurd drama, "present their sense of irrationality of the human condition in the form of highly lucid and logically constructed reasoning, while the theatre of the absurd strives to express its sense of the senselessness of the human condition and the inadequacy of the rational approach by the open abandonment of rational devices and discursive thought. While Sartre or Camus express the new content in the old convention, the theatre of the absurd goes a step further in trying to achieve a unity between its basic assumptions and the form in which these are expressed."[5] Jerome Ashmore in his article published in Modern Drama while tracing the origin of the trend 'absurd' strives to correlate it with different branches of literature. He says, "In Tantalus the 'absurd' is associated with the futility of desires, in Sissyphus it designates the moral doomed to incompleteness, and in Prometheus it exhibits the God's denial of men's claim to parity them."[6]

The term 'Theatre of Absurd' was coined by Hungarian-born critic Martin Esslin for the work of a number of playwrights, mostly written in 1950's and 1960's. The term is derived by the French philosopher Albert Camus in 1942 from his essay The Myth of Sisyphus, in which he defines the human situation as basically meaningless and absurd. Esslin regarded the term "Theatre of the Absurd" merely as a 'device' by which he meant to bring attention to certain fundamental traits discernible in the works of a range of playwrights. The playwrights loosely grouped under the label of the absurd attempted to convey their sense of bewilderment, anxiety and wonder in the face of a pixilated universe. The playwrights of the movement are Eugene Ionesco, Samuel Beckett, Jean Genet, Harold Pinter, Arthur Adamov, Arthur Kopit, Ferdando Arrabal, Edward Albee and a few other playwrights, who were not always comfortable with the label and sometimes preferred to use the terms "Anti-theatre" or "New Theatre"

The Theatre of the Absurd was undoubtedly strongly influenced by the traumatic experience of the horrors of the Second World War, which showed the total impermanence of any values, and highlighted the dangers of human life and its fundamental meaninglessness and arbitrariness. Like the Surrealist and the Dadaist drama that emerged after the First World War, the Theatre of the Absurd, is a product of the post Second World War disillusionment. The barbaric attacks of war disillusioned and made people shift their faith from religion to science. This failure of religion as well as science created a feeling of void, emptiness, rootlessness and an atmosphere of doubt, futility and purposelessness of life.

As a result, absurd plays assumed a highly unusual, innovative form, directly aiming to shock the viewer, shaking him out of this comfortable, conventional everyday life. World War II was the catalyst that finally brought the Theatre of Absurd to life. The 'absurd' drama was quite different from almost all aspects of classical drama which were in vogue. 'Theatre of Absurd' strives to express the senselessness of the human condition and argues about the absurdity of human condition. It merely shows it in terms of the concrete stage images of 'Absurdity' of existence. Martin Esslin asserted the same view saying, "These plays flout all traditional conventional notions, of the plot, character, dialogue, theme, setting, and structure."[7] It openly rebelled against conventional theatre. It was, as Ionesco called 'anti-theatre'. It was surreal, illogical, conflictless and plotless.

The Theatre of Absurd owes as much to German expressionism, as to French surrealism, existentialism, realism and naturalism. The fundamental problem of life and death, isolation and communication, are chiefly dealt within the drama of the 'absurd'. The theme of alienation is the backbone of the drama of the 'absurd.' Man is alienated from the world in the sense that the world he inhabits does not follow him nor does he find his own function in it. The absurd combines the search for concrete in the place of abstract, the forlornness and anxiety of an abandoned individual in chaotic world.

Though the 'absurd' has its origin in different countries of Europe, the main credit can be given to France mainly for the origin of its techniques. The chief contributors of the 'Drama of Absurd' are not French but immigrants. Except Jean Genet, Samuel Beckett, Eugene Ionesco, Arthur, Adamov wrote their plays in French and used the primitive technique do not belong to France. Martin Esslin referring to this says "Beckett used 'Ballets and Mime plays', Eugene Ionesco made use of the 'Proliferation of things and ballets', Jean Genet showed his inclination in the use of 'Ritual and Pure stylized action'. Martin Esslin goes to the extent of saying that "The Theatre of the Absurd is in effect a return to earlier non-verbal forms of Theatre."[8] It is not confined to one particular period, neither is it centered to one particular place, not to one particular technique. It is as ancient as the drama itself. But as a movement, as a genre, it is quite modern and of recent origin.

An appropriate question that confuses the mind of many researchers with regard to the emergence of modern American Drama and the theatre of Absurd is the vague ancestry; say the lineage of contemporary American theatre. The drama of 'absurd' is a type of experiment in the theatre, though experimented by French masters, took America by its stride. 'The New Wave' as stated earlier began with off-off Broadway by a German production of Edward Albee's The Zoo Story, of Jack Gelber's *The Connection* by the living theatre, Harvard University's production of Arthur Kopit's *Oh Dad, Poor Dad, Mama has hung you in the Closet And I am feeling so sad* and *The Prodigal* of Jack Richardson. This group of four American playwrights has shown their concern with the predicament of man in the universe, essentially those summarized by Albert Camus in his philosophic essay '*The Myth of Sisyphus*'.

The sixties seem to be dedicated to a variety of adventures in the new drama of the 'absurd' dealing with the metaphysical anguish of modern man. Edward Albee comes into the Theatre of the Absurd precisely because his work attacks the very foundations of American optimism. For Albee, writing is an 'emotional catharsis'. The metaphysical anguish he experienced and witnessed is dramatized in terms of domestic, social, historical, psychological and philosophical conflicts about nothing in particular. Many plays of Albee reveal the ultimate nothing, the final truth avoided by humanity as a whole and Americans in particular, by such palliative dreams as the family, the nation, the frontier and the race. The Zoo Story presents the quiet courage required to avoid all these cherished ideals and to be human and to face failures in a society in which nothing succeeds like success because the society is dominated by the dollar ethic, commercial morality and utilitarian culture.

Like Sartre, Albee believes that the responsibility of drama is to help modern man recognize the ultimate significance of human life. As a dramatist of human condition, Albee probes into the human psyche and like other contemporary writers, Albee's dramas take the shape of a search for meaning which involves man at every level of his conscious experience. This ceaseless search relays his tragic experience in all its grandeur, splendor and beauty. "Like Goethe whose works form a great confession, Eliot who believes that "what poets starts from is his own emotions" and Pirandello whose "philosophy sprang from deep personal experience, Albee found the matrix of his vision in his own personal history"[9] Albee monitors in his plays the essential sickness of the American soul as also its restlessness and mysterious flights. He explores the possibilities of meaningful existence in a supposedly meaningless universe. The purpose of the genuine "theater of the absurd", as Albee sees it is "to make a man face up to the human condition as it really is ..."[10]

Albee in his first play The Zoo Story 1959 deals essentially with isolation, a common element of life in large cities and of human outcasts in savage society. 'The Zoo' in the The Zoo Story which constitutes the central symbol of the play is an image of human isolation and absence of contact and communication. The play is an encounter between two New York citizens named Jerry and Peter who meet for the first time on a Sunday afternoon. Its two characters-representatives of different social class, constitute a model of American experience as Albee sees it. Peter sitting on a bench in Central park is anxious to avoid human contact at all costs. On the contrary Jerry alarmingly irrational is determined to provoke some response from Peter. The conversation between these two men reveals the social class, intellectual interests, goals and way of life.

Peter has no particular mark to distinguish him from so many thousands of others. He is one of those satisfied bourgeois who leads a comfortable life with, 'one wife, two daughters, two cats and two parakeets.' Peter is the modern version of stereotype of everyman. He reads the 'right books and has the average number of children.' He blends perfectly into the emptiness of the modern landscape. The 'bars' which separate Peter from his own nature and from other people is the material goods and the fabricated ideas with which he surrounds himself. He has carefully constructed his own isolation.

Jerry, a shabby idler, is little younger, in his thirties is not poorly dressed but carelessly dressed. Indeed the description of Jerry could equally be applied to "his sense of an America which has become flaccid and enervated, which has lost its clarity of outlines, its energy and its vision."[11] "What was once a trim and lightly muscled body has', as we are told 'begun to go to fat; and while he is no longer handsome, it is evident that he once was. His fall from physical grace should not suggest debauchery; he has, to come closet to it, a great weariness"[12]. (P. 11) He lives in a rooming house, alone, without family or friends, with his utensils, typewriter, pornographic playing cards, empty picture frames, unanswered and unanswerable letters. He finds it impossible to have an extended relationship with a woman. He is physically sickened by his landlady, the only person who wants to have contact with him. She is "fat, ugly, mean, stupid, unwashed misanthropic, cheap, drunken bag of garbage" (P. 33) who presses her disgusting body against him.

Jerry attempts to convert Peter to his new religion of love and relationship and contact with fellow beings. He attempts a number of strategies. Since language is devoid of its real meanings filled with clichés, Jerry is forced to adopt a more oblique approach. He begins his story of the dog, explaining that "sometimes it is necessary to go a long distance out of the way in order to come back a short distance correctly. (P. 36) When his simple conversation fails to reach Peter, Jerry resorts to a parable, narrating the story of his relationship with his landlady's dog whose relationship ultimately parallels the one existing between him and Peter. Peter serves as audience to Jerry's story on the stage just as the audience in the Theatre. "The story of the dog" provides an opportunity to observe the more recent pattern of Jerry's actions as he attempts to forge a new bond. He justifies this attempt as "a person has to have some way of dealing with SOMETHING. If not people ... if not with people ... with SOMETHING: "A dog. It seemed like a perfectly sensible idea. Man is a dog's best friend". (pp. 42-43) Peter's first reaction is to say that he does not understand and later he asserts to say, "I don't want to HEAR ANYMORE, I don't understand you, or your landlady, or her dog" (P. 45)

Failing to deter Peter, Jerry at last resorts to a more desperate device - claiming the whole bench for him: 'a bench to which Peter retreats in order to escape from those people who are the source of his own anxieties and which thus come to stand as an image of his self-imposed isolation.' Jerry provokes him further to defend his bench as the dog provoked him to kill in spite of his love towards it. He tells Peter, "I went to the Zoo to find out more about the way people exist with animals, the way animals exist with each other, and with people too". (P. 49) Jerry pokes him on his arm at which Peter is naturally annoyed. Gradually, at Jerry's strange behavior, he was 'very much annoyed, flabbergasted and flustered'. He says:

> But ... whatever for? What is the matter with you? Besides, I see no reason why I should give up this bench. I sit on this bench almost every Sunday afternoon, in good weather. It's secluded here; there's never anyone sitting here, so I have it all to myself. (pp. 51-52)

No longer could Peter brook Jerry's poking and punching. They could only provoke animal nature in him. But Jerry has decided once and for all. He has come to the central park with the purpose of sacrificing his life for the sake of making contact with his fellow beings. He throws a knife to Peter to fight with him and then deliberately impales himself on it on a sudden thought.

Jerry would have probably been saved from his doom. But Peter's failure stems from the fact that he never dared to confront the reality of his life and in this sense Peter too is as helpless as Jerry himself is. Bigsby also agrees when he says "For Peter is not only brought into a new and more meaningful relationship with reality but is introduced to the need for the genuine human contact which is anti-thesis of absurdity"[13]

The play is paradoxical in nature. It expresses that cruelty is part of love. One cannot reach others without hurting them sometimes, and one cannot reach himself without experiencing some pain. Slykes comments:

> The particular insights -the inevitability, even the necessity for cruelty and pain, the superiority of hostility to indifference are of particular importance in understanding the reminder of the play. Albee in this play as in other plays advocates the need of love without which human relations turn beastly and which is not possible here on earth.[14]

The 'extraordinary violence' resides in the fact that in modern life the very concept of love has been distorted and corrupted and that both the halves of polarized society are equally incapable of communication. Albee has drawn both Peter and Jerry on similar lines; both are lonely and imprisoned in their skins. The gestures of love are totally lacking in the society and this is seen in Jerry where he is found surrounded by material things which are incomplete and symbolize and reinforce the incompleteness and unnatural predicament or impotent modern man who cannot love. It also raises another critical problem. When an alienated man finds himself incapable of overcoming separateness, he turns to violence in a last desperate effort to establish some perversion of love which is the only alternative whereby modern man can bridge the gap between the polarities of unity and communication. It also reveals that the loneliness and the emptiness of the characters as the result of the collapse of values in the Western world in general and in the United States in particular.

Charles Lyons says "The Zoo Story is within the genre classification of the absurd ... because it assumes the absurdity, chaos of the human condition and its essential loneliness."[15] And Gilbert Debusscher states thus "It belongs to the pessimistic, defeatist or nihilistic current which characterizes the entire contemporary theatrical scene."[16]

The Death of Bessie Smith presents the racial conflict between the Whites and Blacks. This play may be called an anti-social absurd drama, like *Deathwatch,* with a real tragic poignancy of the kind we find in the *Death of a Salesman.* The absurd drama has neither plot nor theme and in The Death of Bessie Smith there is neither plot nor development of the situation but it rather provokes the racial prejudice of the time.

> What is most alarming ... is that the whole idea ... of a life dedicated to the values that cannot be realized by a commercial civilization ... has lost its allure.[17]

Albee is struck by the emptiness of the modern civilization. The barriers of class, race, religion and politics put people into cages which close them off from the possibility of growth which will enable them to live fully and really. For, instance, by creating convincing dramatic situations, Albee communicated through The Death of Bessie Smith, the horrors of civilization that has lost its human contact and reality. The emotional insufficiency of the individual and the pressures of the society that distorts the real response to life are substantiated through a social injustice, namely racism. As such the play explains how the institution, whether a private family or a public hospital are often misunderstood and misused. Death of Bessie Smith presents racism only as a symptom but not as a disease.

Albee makes use of the legend about the death of the famous Blues singer to explore the evil effects of racial discrimination, an inhuman practice nourished by the people. But there is a difference in the way Albee looks at the problem. His is not the politics of racism but the humanism of it. The Intern's self-explanation can be taken as the view of the author: "I am not concerned with politics ... But I have a sense of urgency ... a dislike of waste ... stagnation." [P.110] Mainly the play is about the collapse of human values and national purpose. In other words as Stenz observes, it is an

> ...exploration of the effects which the rigid institutions have on the development of the individual ... is particularly concerned with the consequences for everyone involved in a climate of living which fosters racism".[18]

The central idea of the play is when Jack tries to admit the Negro Blues singer, Bessie Smith in a hospital. The injuries proved fatal when she was turned away by "Mercy" hospital only for 'Whites'. Thus Albee, at the first instance itself, ironically delivers the meaning of the term 'mercy' by which the hospital is called. The crux of the issue is that Bessie Smith's life might have been saved had she been immediately hospitalized. The same theme is infused into the main plot as a mark of reiteration which indicates how Albee is deeply struck by the pressures of the society that dictate the life of an individual.

A subtle analysis of the characters show the conflict between each character's longing for growth and self-expression and the inhibiting influence of the institutional demands. Their 'life begins to parody itself and the essence of parody lies in its power to diminish;' and so 'the human experience is not best defined by pain but by loss.' Paul Witherington observes: "the imagery of the play is built around the desire for movement and change on the one hand and stasis on the other".[19]

The plot of the play rotates round the Nurse. All the dramatic personae in the play get significance because they are related to her. The Nurse's lover is a White Knight, a liberal thinker who is pinning to participate in Spanish Civil War. At the hospital there is a Negro Orderly who torments the nurse by pointing out the corruption of her heritage. Next is her cigar chomping, racist, semi-invalid father. Though the life of her father has been very fashionable and prosperous in 'Dixie fashion', she hates him. Father and daughter are highly irritable, suspicious and mean ready to hurt each other to the utmost. The name of Bessie Smith seems imaginary only. She is either historical or a popular figure. She never appears on the stage though the title of the play bears her name. The play appears to be split into several parts: that dealing with Bessie and Jack and the other dealing with Nurses' affairs at the hospital.

The Nurse is a pathetic character. She hits everyone around her yet she never escapes from her cage. The cage symbolizes the separation which cages are furnished with. The Nurse repeats the phrase out in a howl of protest directed at the Intern and at life in general, "I'm tired of ... world", (P. 36) a number of times, yet there is no better place for her to go to. She says:

> "I'm sick of everything in this hit stupid fly-ridden world, I'm sick of the disparity between things as they are, and as they should be! ... I am tired ...I'm tired of the truth ... I am tired of lying about the truth ...I'm tired of my skin, ... I WANT OUT!" (pp. 124 -25)

The Nurse feels tired of being toyed with. She is 'sick of' the talks of the Intern but she is not able to get away from the boredom which he has created around her or she is put into. The torments which the Nurse faces in her life due to varied reasons are directed, by her towards Negro Orderly. Albee does not clarify why Orderly submits to her. The absurdist supplies elements in a confusing manner. The beholder usually is left to make sense out of them; the audience is supposed to create a meaning for the play. The play has a problem which is presented by Intern. The problem is "How is a man to fulfill himself?" (P. 38) A question like this smells more of philosophy and less of the drama and it forms the basis of this 'absurd' play.

The dilemma of the Orderly is contrary to his conscience, he falls in line with the mass order; because he could do nothing but serve in the hospital. His failure to resolve this dilemma is hopelessly absurd. Thoroughly conditioned by the dominant society, the Orderly half believes he is what she makes him to be, instead of what he feels himself capable of becoming. Nurse comes down in abuse towards the Orderly, she has a subconscious sexual desire for the Orderly, which reveals the supremacy of the Whites who utilize the service of the Negroes for their selfish ends. The Orderly tries to please everybody but only succeeds in isolating himself from all. The dialogue of the Orderly throughout the play is broken or unfinished phrases; because his manliness is plucked away by the social discrimination. Whose fault is it to be born a Negro? God's or mans'?

Intern, a liberal thinker is caught in a dilemma of choice between his physical or sexual love for the Nurse and his conviction of indispensability of his service in the Spanish war. The cruel death of Bessie Smith makes the Intern to leave the hospital and the Nurse. Though he is fascinated towards the Nurse he is still his own man. His interest in people, in the basic humanity, his compassion and love are realistically focused. He stands as model to all. He is of the opinion that if there arises any conflict between preserving the law and human life, life should have consideration.

Contrary to the opinion expressed by Gilbert Debauccer that "not one character is capable of extracting meaning from the Jazz singer's death".[20] The significance of the play lies in the optimism. Albee infuses his optimism of life, in his delineation of the character, the Intern, who only lives up to the values of individual's conscience, remaining ideal and challenging model. As Allan Lewis points out "The play is not altogether a drama of helpless and hopeless lives".[21] Intern breaks out of the vicious cycle of desire for change compounded with inertia. It is through the Intern the essential purpose of the play is achieved.

The play The Death of Bessie Smith seems more social, more racial and an oversimplified protest drama in its treatment of the general inhumanity of the White towards Negro reflected in Bessie's needless death. The protest is expressed on the part of the Negro to get entrance in the White's hospital, and when entrance is denied they prefer to meet death rather than going to another hospital. The play relates itself to the tradition of the 'absurd' in its treatment of inaction. The plays of the 'absurd' believe neither in action nor in conversation. In Scene II of the play, the Nurse and her father are seen arguing about their car. This intention appears thirteen times. But we see no indication of the car being used either by the Nurse or by the father, and she accuses her father for merely watching the car. "You are going to sit with a shotgun and make sure the birds do not crap on it" (P. 33) In Scene I, Jack is going to go up to north, but he cannot resist sitting instead with his friend and talk about going. Bessie is lying on the bed throughout Scene III while Jack tries to get her up and move. In Scene V a meaningless gossipy telephone conversation between the two Nurses is seen. In all the characters in the play the Nurse alone appears to be able to execute her purpose better than the other characters that live in fear of her power. Thus all the characters in the play are going to do something but execution is always lacking. Besides lack of action in the play, there can be heard Beckettian notes in the futility of action. In Becketts *Waiting for Godot* waiting and moving prove futile. In The Death of Bessie Smith, also neither waiting nor moving can be seen in Bessie. Paul Withrington also expresses the similar views when he says, "The fact that Bessie has been dead for sometime reveals that the drama is not about a particular emergency or about Negro and White as such but about larger issue of human commitment".[22] It is the larger issue of human that the play bothers through out and it is this concern that relates the Bessie Smith to the' absurd'.

In the tradition of the Theatre of the Absurd, The Sandbox (1960) is Albee's comment on the treatment of death and dying in America, and the ridiculousness of waiting to expire. A woman's advanced age signals her imminent death, and her daughter and son-in-law deposit her on a beach and impatiently wait for her to die. She longs for their affection but suffers their indifference, and so discloses her life story to the audience.

Mommy "a well dressed and imposing woman" of fifty-five years and Daddy "a small thin and grey man" who is sixty years old, and Grandma who is eighty-six years old are examples of the absurdity of a modern middle-class family of America which is sterile and cruel. The background is the sky in the seashore which alters from brightest day to deepest night which is symbolic and sets the tone of the plays. The play's action is concerned with the disposal of Grandma by her ruthless daughter and spineless son-in-law. Grandma, a tiny, wizened woman with bright eyes, easily represents the old rural values of the waning generation which is being flaunted in the modern marriage of the urban Mommy and Daddy. Mommy and Daddy have decided to do away with Grandma by dumping her in a sandbox to die of cold. The feelings of concern, love and kindness are missing in their family. Finally Grandma, with contentment and resignation, gets herself acquainted with death in the hands of the Angel of Death. Making a mockery of the whole affair of keeping a watch over Grandma's dying, Mommy and Daddy are satisfied that they have done their duty. Mommy is depicted as a vain, hollow being who wears the pants in the house and takes all the decisions. It is her decision to dispose Grandma off; she chooses the place suitable for this purpose. She directs the musician when to play music and when to stop and it is she who finally decides their time of departure. On the other hand, Daddy is seen as emasculated, submissive, quite opposite of male image in society, who acquiesces to the decision of the Mommy meekly, who has nothing in particular to say to her and who does nothing but whine like a child on feeling either 'cold' or 'hot'.

The theme of abandonment begins graphically as Grandma is being carried by the armpits and dumped into a sandbox. Mommy and Daddy perform it with much fun as if Grandma is a lifeless object. Her 'puzzlement and fear' and her protest Ah-haaaaa! Grandma! is overlooked by the heartless couple. The poor lady is forcibly taken out of the house to be dumped in the sandbox, not by her son-in-law but her own daughter. Grandma addresses the audience:

> What a way to treat an old woman! Drag her out of the house ... stick her in a car ... bring her out here from the city ... dump her in a pile of sand ... and leave her here to set. (P. 149)

The play offers a very example of the drama of the 'absurd' in its treatment of incoherent behavior, lack of meaning in human life, and illogical response to the actions the play shows. Mommy (Brightly) says:

> So it is! Well! Our long night is over; We must pay our tears, take off our mourning ... and face the future. It's our duty. (p. 155)

Albee wrote this 'perfect play' The Sandbox in memory of his grandmother who died in 1959, at the age of eighty-three. While working on The American Dream, Albee received a commission to write a brief play for the Spoleto festival of Two Worlds. So he wrote The Sandbox (1959) which later gave birth to The American Dream whose themes are almost identical. Though it takes thirteen minutes, Albee observes that it is worked out to perfection. Later he revealed his admiration for it: "I'm terribly fond of The Sandbox. I think it's an absolutely beautiful, lovely perfect play."[23]

Recollecting his boyhood experience at Larchmont, he blends the rejection of the old by the heartless generation headed by Mommy and Daddy and his own sympathy for the old represented by Grandma. This is the first play which introduces Mommy and Daddy who stand for "empty affection and point up the pre-senility and vacuity of their characters". (P. 143)

The Sandbox besides being a fine example of the 'absurd' seems to get involved in social problems. Gilbert Debussacher observes that the play deals with "the shameless organized exploitation ... if the survivors who buy peace of mind for the diseased whom they have abused or ignored while they were alive"[24] Luciana P. Gabbard observes that the play comments on society's neglect of both children and the aged. She finds a pattern of abandonment in the first three plays of Albee (i.e) The Zoo Story, The Death of Bessie Smith and The Sandbox. According to her "The Zoo Story deals with class opposition, The Death of Bessie Smith with racial opposition and The Sandbox with opposition between generations. Naturally these 'three plays' move inward from a community of strangers in a New York rooming house and park to a smaller company of co-workers in a Memphis hospital to the basic family unit".[25]

The extension of the play The Sand Box is The American Dream (1960). In fact, they 'were the identical twins ... derived from the same ovum ... but separated' for the world festival. Martin Esslin grouped Albee in the company of European absurdity by including his The Zoo Story in his edition of The Absurd Drama (1959). Again it is he who welcomed The American Dream as "a promising and brilliant first example of an American contribution in the theatre of the absurd"[26] Therefore it is believed that Albee has secured place among the American absurdist's. Ann Paolucci also expressed more or less the same sentiment. According to her, Albee has tried his hand for the first time; "at the idiom of the absurd in a total situation which is a whole series of familiar, everyday confrontations"[27] She praises his moving allegories and cumulative progressions which are gradual from nonsense to logic and statement to ironic implications.

In The American Dream, Albee seems to be continuing the urge, the need for genuine human contact based on a clear perception of the real. Albee's play is dedicated to revealing the inadequacies of American Dream. The play deals with the problems of American society, the disrespect and negligence for the old generation and the hollowness of the relations itself. The play presents five characters - Mommy, Daddy, Grandma, Mrs. Barker and a Young Man. Out of these five dramatic personae the most sensible one seems to be

Grandma in her witty arguments and practical view of life. Like his other plays, The American Dream is a 'one-act abstract Vaudeville sketch." Mommy and Daddy representatives of 'the home' radiate anything but vitality and constructive affection. Their apartment is an emotional void which sterilizes and petrifies the manners and ceremonies of human life. In spite of the number of years that they have shared together there is only emptiness in the lives of Mommy and Daddy. In the opening scene of the play, Mommy and Daddy are being seated together in their decorative living room; waiting for someone to perform apparently some kind of household service which is generally suggestive of the meaningless life they are living. They have nothing substantial to do. Mommy whiles away her time and amuses herself by moving 'from one apartment to another, up and down the social ladder'. She keeps buying hats and other odds and ends and derives 'satisfaction', which she claims Daddy cannot get. "Love becomes impossible and absurdity is accepted as the norm"[28]

The family depicted in the play has all the privileges in terms of wealth but it lacks the substantial part of a family. It adopts a child from some institution, 'Bye-Bye Adoption' through a lady known as Mrs.Barker. Afterwards this child does not come up to the expectation of Mommy and Daddy who leave the child crippled by mauling its hands, legs and finally the eyes. But after a few years the couple again shows inclination for adopting another child and a Young Man appears there who exactly the person the couple needed is. The Young Man enters this family at the time when Mommy had been preparing to put the Grandma in a nursing home. Thus the forced disappearance of Grandma and the arranged appearance of the Young Man offer a sharp contrast as well as the unease on the part of young generation. It depicts the conflict between the old and young. The young generation is getting restless to oust old generation. Albee in the preface to The American Dream says, 'The purpose of the play is, to offend -as well as amuse and entertain, and every honest work is a personal, private yowl, a statement of an individual pleasure and pain'.

Thus The American Dream observes the individual pleasure and pain and presents the personal involvement that inspires Albee's attacks. However, this involvement removes him from close kinship with social dramatist and draws him closer to August Strindberg and Tennessee Williams in his inclination for sexual conflicts and use of symbols. Albee does not like to name his characters. He feels satisfied to call them after the position in the family and then in the society. The adopted child is called 'bubble'.

The drama of the 'absurd' belongs to the experimental theatre where all the conventional and traditional themes are declared out -dates when reality is not a thing of craze and need and where genuine feelings are reduced to sentimentality. Here only the expression of reality is enough. The play deals with the notion that human feelings like pity, affection and love give way to a cold, clinical rationalization where the value of marriage is not much better than commercial. Mommy tells Daddy, "We were poor but then I married you Daddy, and we became rich". (p. 22) Mommy in return supplies physical demands of Daddy. This give and take policy is working in all the relations in the world.

Their statements of affection for each other, "You're my sweet Daddy", and "I love you Mommy" sound empty and meaningless and are uttered for the sake of saying something. Mommy has never treated Daddy or the child as human beings with individual needs and desires separate from her, but rather as instrument through which to gain satisfaction which is mainly self-aggrandizing. They are both necessary for her as she would lose her identity and purpose of life without them; she needs them both for her social status. It would be a misinterpretation of the author's overall intention to describe Mommy as 'emancipate' as Rutenberg does. She is horrible but she is also a brilliant at commenting satirically on the product of a society which encourages woman to believe that marriage and motherhood are the only solutions to the problem of living.

The sterility of this couple suggests the sterility of modern society which is inhibited by spiritually castrated emasculated men and women who live death-in-life. The partner's inability to procreate is an important contributor in the aggravation of the feelings of impotence, guilt, insecurity and inferiority which prevent them from leading happy, peaceful lives. It is also responsible for the absence of communication between the two. The arrival of the second 'bumble' at the end of the play becomes another impediment to communication between Mummy and Daddy as Mother goes into ecstasies over the arrival of the second child and falls over him in order to be acquainted with him and in return, remind him of the happy times she had with the other one. Daddy is sadly pushed aside and fills in the role of spectator for the second time.

The beauty and specialty of the play, The American Dream lies in its expression of absurdity. It offers 'fitfully amusing travesty and sexy young man whose power of love has been destroyed'. The play depicts a family without understanding and shows a contact without communication. These qualities represent an average American family where love, affection and respect are conspicuous by their absence. This child the family adopts is called 'bumble' rather than a baby; and it is smashed and dismembered by the family. As Grandma says:

> Of course, and then, as it got bigger, they found out all sorts of terrible things about it, like: it did not have a head, in its shoulders, it had no guts; it was spineless, its feet were made of clay … just dreadful thing. (P. 62)

In this vacuum enters the American Dream, in the person of a tall, good looking boy, a 'perfect' juvenile specimen'. He had no feeling, no active desires, and no real ambition. He is adopted by Mommy and Daddy to under go the same treatment as the earlier "bumble". The Young Man is "profile, straight nose, honest ears, wonderful eyes" (P. 70). In this sense the title of the play is well-chosen by the playwright.

Albee who seems content merely with the sketch in the details of an "absurd" society here in this play examines the alternative to confrontation. The alternatives are endeavored to supply in the form of the Young Man to get rid of the emptiness, prevailing in the family in the absence of a child and then by putting Grandma in the nursing home.

Like a good representative of absurd tradition, he had discovered that the stage must be made to articulate. Albee has never succumbed to the temptation of using the stage for indignant social commentary, but he has used the stage for social purposes. Besides expressing his view for social set-up, Albee insists on attacking 'on the substitution of artificial for real values in our society'(preface of the play)

Albee's play comparatively less known than his other plays is Seascape (1975) which has won him, his second Pulitzer prize. In tracing the evolution of this evolution play, Albee thought of writing two one-act plays-companion pieces called "Life" and "Death". "Death" began to have a life of its own; which grew into a full-length play, the All Over and his other play "Life" is Seascape, an independent 'four-character' play.

Seascape like Arthur Miller's *The Creation of the World and the other Business* is best regarded as "a consciously naïve attempt to trace human imperfection to its source by unwinding the process of history and myth."[29] George Oppenheimer's says that

> This is Edward Albee's finest play, is patent nonsense. His language is mannered without the tension and the resonance of his earlier work. Meaning is explicit. Events are drained of that very tactile reality which is the essence of the experience on which Nancy wishes to rebuild their lives. The characters exist on the boundaries of land and sea, past and future, pre-history and history, even and emotion, but their very abstraction makes the final reconciliation and optative mood unconvincing.[30]

Albee suggestively described it as a play 'about evolution'. He felt that 'commentators who obstinately concentrate on the familial struggles in his plays ignore the fact that he writes in a wider context: a society, a way of life, even a species. Seascape is an important development in this process and treats the question of the future of the species'. Albee as a social critic and a dramatist is concerned with the conditions with which 'civilized man' lives, where communication hinders his cultural development. He holds that in the absurd world man is caught between his unlimited potential and his awareness of death, the pain of life and the final futility of all action.

The Seascape is a paradox of human predicament "man though he is aware that he is more than an animal, is conscious of the fact that he never ceases to be an animal however civilized he may be or thinks he is. And at the same time, he is aware that he has always something undeniably human about him even in the most primitive stages of his development. Otherwise man could not have evolved into a man."[31] The two couples presented in the Seascape one modern and the other uncivilized and strange, effectively project this innate paradox of human existence. The fundamental contradictoriness is perhaps basically due to the inseparable combination at any stage, of man and beast in every human being.

With Seascape, Albee seems to have moved to a more purely Beckettian world. It is set amidst a stretch of sand but the ironies are pressed in different direction. Although the influence of Beckett is evident in the play by barren setting and its insistent concern with mortality, it is clear that Albee has had a far more optimistic vision. From the character of Nancy, we are reminded that the inevitability of death does not require one to prematurely surrender to its power. Instead Nancy insists that life has to be lived all the way thorough even in old age; in the expectation that there will always be something new and worth experiencing. She is justified in her faith in life's endless promise by the arrival of the lizards, absolutely unanticipated and absolutely enthralling bonanza cast in their laps by the sea.

While unlimited potential and his awareness of death, the pain of life and the final futility of all action is the central theme in all Albee's plays, he attempts to examine whether this consciousness is a curse or blessing in his new play - a fairy tale Seascape. Replacing the sterile world in the body of his works, Albee for the first time has created a couple - Charlie and Nancy - who have given birth to three children and they in turn have produced children of their own. They are happy and contented. The following conversation and the family sentiment seen in the couple is not found in any other couple in Albee's earlier plays:

Charlie: You're a good wife

Nancy: You have been a good husband ... more or less.

Charlie: Damned right

Nancy: And you courted me the way I wanted.

Charlie: Yes.

Nancy: And you gave me the children I wanted, as many, and when. (pp. 29-30)[32]

While Charlie and Nancy are discussing their 'mid-life crisis' what looks like a meaningless chat between the couple about nothing in particular, of emotions like love, of negative feelings like fear, hatred and apprehension, civilized customs like marriage and bringing up children; they encounter strange creatures from the deep sea having a lizard look. They are the primordial lizards whose names are Leslie and Sarah. They arouse curiosity in them and Nancy is fascinated by the lizards as Eve was by the beauty of Satan. The whole situation appears to be absurd. This strange encounter and negotiation between these two couples acts as a catalyst to probe into deep mysteries of nature and life which is difficult to explain.

In creating a naked couple with tails and bringing them into dramatic encounter with an ultramodern couple, Albee has synthesized a perfect fable for projecting the paradox of human situation. Albee described the strange couple Leslie and Sarah as "not human", but as "not-people". "It's I suppose about evolution, really. Two of the characters are people and two of the characters are not ... I'm not saying they're human; they're not people. See the play and find out"[33] The couple, who are 'not-people' with whom the animal imagery is grafted, may be taken to stand for the under-developed, more euphemistically, 'developing people, pestered by problems of population explosion, malnutrition, lack of housing, clothing, uncared for children, hunger and exploitation and other evils of that kind.

Seascape is obviously not a realistic play but it is away from modern frustration and venom. Encounters between human beings and talking animals are the stuff of fairy tales, a work which teaches about inner problems through symbols and communicates various depths of meaning to various levels of personality at various times. Lucina P. Grobbord has interpreted the meaning of the world of 'Seascape' from a new perspective:

> A seascape is a view of the sea whose ever-moving water are the meeting place between air and ground, heaven and earth, life and death. The waters of the sea are both the source and goal of life. Returning to sea is like returning to the birth waters of mother's womb ... The sea is also deep and dark; beneath its bright ripples and under currents, eddies, unseen life, and unplumbed deaths.[34]

Therefore, we can derive that Seascape inter wines with the three levels of meaning: the waters of life, the flux of life, and man's awareness of the bruises of unconscious life. All these are 'condensed in the symbols of the saurian lizards which again remind us of man's emergence of the individual embryo from its watery womb'.

It is this fault and incomplete awareness of life that the existentialist dealt so fondly with and which later, got full expression in the plays of the absurd. Seascape offers an improvement on the absurd tradition as it maintains a balance between the 'surd' and the 'absurd'. The message of the play is 'individual human growth is an analogous to the evolution of mankind. The developmental stages are gradual but inevitable'. The play shows a belief in "no change". Sarah says "Leslie always had a tall" (P. 22) and that their discomfort under the sea was "a growing thing nothing abrupt"(P. 24) The playwright's extreme interest in making love is found in the talks of the couples Charlie and Nancy, Leslie and Sarah. Charlie asks Sarah what she would do if she knew Leslie "was never coming back" (P. 129) and Sarah says "she would cry her eyes out if she lost Leslie" (P. 130)

Harold Clurman calls the play "delightful as well as drag. In either case it is not something that calls for a hysterical reaction. It's a step in Albee's still green career"[35] Jack knoll however holds the following views about the play Seascape. He says:

> In this new play Seascape, Edward Albee seems drained of almost all vitality theatrical, intellectual, artistic and vitality was always Albee's bottom line, the one quality that even his detractors admitted that he possessed.[36]

The ending of the play is commendable. "All right, Begin" which contains the central theme of the play is said by Leslie. Both the couples are now ready to begin the death of the old life so as to be born new. Leslie and Sarah will die to be reborn as human beings because they have gained consciousness of the life of the sea to a middle ground of earth. Charlie and Nancy will die to be reborn to a higher plane of existence in the upper world of air. 'Begin' also suggests, the start of total reconciliation of all conflicting elements of the self - the past with the present, the sub-conscious with the conscious' which allows Seascape to emerge as a benign comedy.

The most conspicuous element in Albee's The Man Who Had Three Arms is how 'fame' which is short lived takes a toll on the individuals when it begins to wane. The play is an angry satire on unearned celebrity that evaporates when the eponymous man loses his third arm. It examines how celebrity status confers illusion of grandeur on individuals, largely encouraged by the media and can be called a ridiculous, absurd play. As Albee states in an interview with Roundane "If any play that I've written that is linked to the Theatre of Absurd, it may very well be The Man Who Had Three Arms. The entire structure of what happens to Himself is based totally on absurdity; and it is precisely the absurdity that he's railing against."[37]

Albee's The Man Who Had Three Arms, with 'Himself' as the protagonist has bold and open assault on the audience. Himself fixed behind the podium, lectures his invisible audience for two acts, presenting his own ethical conflicts directly to both an imagined and real audience. Himself launches a verbal attack not on an unsuspecting Peter or a Nick and Honey or an anesthetized Tobias or a retiring Charlie, but on his audience. For better or worse, the play's audience stands as the recipient of the violence.

Albee discussed this point, observing the relatedness of the actors and audience within his theory of drama:

> In nine or ten of my plays, you'll notice, actors talk directly to the audience. In my mind, this is a way of involving the audience into participation. It may have a reverse effect; some audiences don't like this; they get upset by it quite often; it may alienate them. But I am trying very hard to involve them. I don't like the audience as voyeur, the audience as passive spectator. I want the audience as participant. In that sense, I agree with Artaud: that sometimes we should literally draw blood. I am very fond of doing that because voyeurism in the theatre lets people off the hook. The Man Who Had Three Arms is a specific attempt to do this. It is an act of aggression. It's probably the most violent play I've written.[38]

The Man Who Had Three Arms is an absurdity case study of a sensation-hungry and fickle public being created by a ruthless media by the 'publicity intellectuals' as Saul Bellow would refer to them. Arthur Miller has superbly delineated the fate of the Salesman, Willy Loman; who experienced the fickleness of the Capitalistic system in his play, *Death of a Salesman*. This is the tragic predicament of the absurdly portrayed protagonist -Himself in this play of Albee. Mathew C Roudane has described it as a 'monologue of cruelty' and drawn attention to the Pirandellian nature of the play.

Himself's life took the predictable course of an ordinary, bright, ambitious Youngman, "more than a little curious about the world around him and cosmopolite" shrewd and talented, he went up the ladder in advertising as did Peter in The Zoo Story. He married, had children early and there was nothing but joy and accomplishments, security and predictability and planned easy life and easy cease. Then an event happened which changed his life forever, created him, destroyed him, raised him up and brought him there before the audience. It was his third arm which took him to fame and his world began to fall apart soon after it started diminishing The crowd grew less and less as his arm began to vanish. The Colonel, now a rich man, took the insurance money and left without leaving a trace of him to Himself who is now a totally disillusioned man.

Albee explores the corrupting and transitory effect of "celebrity-hood" - on the top of fortune's wheel one moment and brings it down to the bottom the next moment. Himself experiences financial as well as spiritual bankruptcy and near the close of the play he specifically reflects on the loss of his self. The Intensity of his loss on self can be measured by his hostility towards the audience which is apparently his form of feeling guilty. Disassociated from his self and the other, Himself closes the play with 'a loving plea to stay, a hateful cry to leave, a pitiful gesture to understand'. He begs the audience thus:

> ... I want an apology for all the years!! For all the humiliation ... stay with me. Don't ... leave me alone! Don't leave me! Don't ... leave me alone. (pp. 102-3)

Roudane sums up the play: "Himself represents the latest Albee's hero who has the courage to face life without absurd illusion"[39] Himself wallows in self-pity about his sad story at the end that he is no different from the rest of the common humanity. "I'm just like everyone you know, you love them; you love me. Stop treating me like a freak! I'm not a freak! I am you. I have always been you! I am you !!! Stop looking at me !! Like that!! [P. 102]

Albee as a social critic exploits the myth of the American Dream in The Man Who Had Three Arms. In an interview with Roudane he said: "...In this play I have very carefully created a monster, Himself, who rose to incredible fame without any ability of is own, besides the fact that he grew a third arm, which is hardly a talent, an accomplishment. It's merely something that happened. And he is taken up by the press, by the media, and is built into this false god. I was examining the way in which we worship that which is wrong: the way we worship that which is empty and artificial; and the way we devour and spit out."[40]

Albee's characters are charged with not only demonstrating the absurdity of a particular society but also the absurdity of the human condition in general. The American Dream and The Sandbox reveal the tragic absurdity of the cherished values of American life, symbolically represented by an athletic youth drained of all feelings, human emotions and values and the paralyzed living-death of the three generations of American life telescoped into one family. Albee explodes the shallowness of well-reasoned metaphysics and the theologically ordered vision of existence in Tiny Alice. Albee shackles the absurdities of life, its inequalities and heinousness. He also focuses his microscope upon it, and leaves us to react. Tiny Alice forces the readers to question and to ponder. Albee tries to pluck the masks from life and death, sex, love and marriage, God, faith and organized religion, money-greed, wealth, charity and even celibacy.

Albee has ably handled the main theme of American family life by transforming the contradiction into evasion. He explodes the myth of happy American family in plays like A Delicate Balance, Counting the Ways, All Over and Three Tall Women. While the modern man evades facing the real home issues, he attempts to build up a 'home' on sandy grounds of illusion. As far as he remains in the illusory home life, all is well, but once it is broken, he feels exposed to reality, which is unbearable and absurd. Marriage, diminution and sex in Tiny Alice, A Delicate Balance and Finding the Sun, confronts Albee's own issues about sexuality with the feeling of frustration in which he shows love to be just a simulacrum.

Box and Quotations are two inter-related plays which stand by themselves and can be enacted one without the other. The out-growth of Box is Quotations From Chairman Mao-Tse-tung. The invisible voice is the articulate expression of a crone which comes from the nearby spectator. The images, the voice used, the stories it tells are of moral depravity of everything in the modern world. The emptiness and hollowness of life is delineated in the account of wealthy lady, who offers a picture of futility and emptiness of the middle-class world. The absurd point comes here, "The play with a recorded voice presents a tiresome threnody on human predicament and the degree to which art can serve as a solace as well as a spus."[41]

In Box, the woman never appears on the stage like Virginia Woolf and Bessie. Bessie is more disturbing in her death than in her life, similarly the invisible lady is more troubling in her absence than she would have been in her presence. In the Quotations From Chairman Mao-Tse-tung the absurd points are apparent. The Old - Woman recites stanza after stanza, from Will Careleton's *Over the Hills to the Poor House*. She is left alone and nobody listens to her. He who is supposed to listen cannot respond. The difficulty of communication is always there. The play combines paradoxical characteristics in its treatment of measuring life in terms of loss, and contact is judged by its absence.

The most valuable innovation the absurdists have introduced into the modern theatre is that they insist gestures in dramatic art. Like Artaud, Albee makes use of mime and pantomime in the Vaudevillian tradition in his twin plays, Counting the Ways and Listening, in which he attempts to use a language that goes deeper than a spoken language-a language that speaks directly to our senses than to the mind. As Box and Quotations From Chairman Mao-Tse-tung are the compilation of Mao's political writings and the verses of an old ballad, Counting the Ways is a random collection of skits. As a true absurdist in an American way, he replaces the central action by creating a series of situations, bringing together the loose, unconnected situations; he builds up his play from centrifugal to centripetal position. Albee deliberately makes use of the so-called formlessness just to reflect the play's subject matter, which is the state of modern marriage. Albee strongly believes that a romantic love and marriage in the modern era are essentially hollow, empty and devoid of any substance and meaning. That is why he uses the functional names like Mommy and Daddy in The American Dream and The Sandbox and He and She in Counting the Ways and Man and Woman in the Listening.

Death, in fact has been a running character through out Albee's works. Albee's ongoing concern with that most significant relationship of all -between one's choices in life and the inevitability of one's death is shown in All Over, The Lady from Dubuque and Three Tall Women. His plays centre around death at three levels; those who have died those who are dying and those who are dead to life. As in Pirandello, here death is a mirror, reflecting family ties built upon rancor, resentment and rivalry. Albee sees failure of love and divorce as a form of dying and killing. In All Over, the whole play talks about the death of the dying man but we are aware of the fact that the persons who are around him are already 'dead' in their flesh and spirit and so they are dying a death invariably.

The constant themes in Albee's plays, telling the urgency to connect and embrace life beyond the absurd, can be seen in Fragments, The Play about the Baby and Occupant. Bigsby insists that Albee's central motif is to do with the belief in life's 'awful futility' and 'amazing wonder.' The Goat or Who is Sylvia? Albee's latest play is a violent, bestial, American family, which is shown only to better question the false normative values of modern civilization and man's alienation to nature. Martin, the protagonist of the play is in a world where there are no rules and where he is tormented by love of 'an unimaginable kind'. Like A Delicate Balance, one of Albee's three Pulitzer Prize winning dramas, The Goat or Who is Sylvia ? tears down boundaries between realism and absurdism.

From all the plays of Albee we can conclude that he uses' Vaudeville' as the vehicle to show how man relies on isolation and illusion to cope with life. The gestures of love, sexual attraction, parental affection, family feeling and hospitality remain, but the actual feelings which would give these gestures a poignant meaning have gone. In his plays the characters are isolated from each other in little words of selfishness, impotence and lovelessness and all warmth of human contact is sterility. Albee implies that the sterility which the audience sees and feels in his characters is typical of the society as a whole, and is created and perpetuated by the society. His characters are charged not only with demonstrating the absurdity of a particular society but also the absurdity of the human condition in general.

REFERENCES

1. Dr. Nageswar Rao G: Preface, *Encounter with nothing* S.V.University Press, Tirupati 1979.
2. Martin Esslin, *Introduction to Absurd Drama* (Harmonds Worth, Penguin Books Ltd., 1976), p. 7.

3. Martin Esslin, *The Theatre of the Absurd* (Penguin Books, London, March 1961), p. 23.
4. Martin Esslin, *The Theatre of Absurd* (Penguin Books is Association with Eyre & Spothis Woodes, London (March 1961), P. 23.
5. *Ibid.* p. 23.
6. Jerome Ashmore, *Interdisciplinary Roots of the Theater of the Absurd*, Modern Drama, in Vol. 14, No. 1 (1971), pp. 72-83.
7. Martin Esslin, *Introduction to Absurd Drama* (Harmodsworth, Penguin Books Ltd., 1976), p. 7.
8. Martin Esslin, *The Theatre of the Absurd* (New York Grove Press, 1961), p. 319.
9. C.P.Singh, *Edward Albee: The playwright of Quest*, Vittal Publications, Delhi 1987) p. 2.
10 Albee, *Which Theatre is the Absurd One?* p. 31 as Quoted in Richard E.Amacher, "Edward Albee", Twayne Publishers, Inc.: New York.
11. C.W.E Bigsby, *A Critical Introduction to Twentieth Century American Drama*, Cambridge: Cambridge University Press, 1984. p. 257.
12. Edward Albee:, *The Zoo Story, The Death of Bessie Smith, The Sandbox*. New York: Coward –McCann, 1960. (All Further References are made from this Text).
13. C.W.E. Bigsby, *Confrontation and Commitment*, (Columbia University of Missouri Press, 1968) , p. 75.
14. Carole, A.Slykes, *Albee's Beast Fables: The Zoo Story and A Delicate Balance*; Educational Theatre Journal Vol. 25 (December 1973), pp. 448-455.
15. Charles Lyons, *Two Projections of the isolation of the human: Brencht's I'm Dickicht Der and Albee's The Zoo Story,* Drama Survey IV (1965) p. 13.
16. Gilbert Debusscher, *Edward Albee: Tradition and Renewal* Trans. A.D.Williams (Brussels, 1967), p. 82.
17. Irving Howe, *A World More Attractive: A View of Modern Literature and Politics* (New York: 1965), p. 256.
18. Anita Maria Stenz, *Edward Albee: The Poet of Loss* (The Hague: Mouton, 1978), p. 14.
19. Paul Withreington, *Language of Movement in Albee's The Death of Bessie Smith*, Twentieth Century Litt., 13, No. 2 (July 1867), p. 86.

20. Gilbert Debauccer, *Edward Albee: Tradition and Renewal*, p. 28.
21. Allan Lewis, *Fun and Games of Edward Albee*, American Plays and Playwrights in the Contemporary Theatre. (New York: Crown Publishers, Inc, 1965), p. 85.
22. Paul Withreington, *Language of Movement in Albee's The Death of Bessie Smith*, Twentieth Century Litt., 13, No. 2 (July 1867), p. 86.
23. William Flannagan, *Edward Albee: An Interview in Writers at Work*, 3rd Series (New York: Viking Press, 1967), p. 346.
24. Gilbert Debauccer, *Edward Albee: Tradition and Renewal*, p. 30.
25 Luciana P. Gabbard, *Edward Albee's: Triptych on Abandonment*, Twentieth Century Literature, 28, (Spring 1983), p. 28.
26. Martin Esslin, *The theatre of the Absurd* (Penguin Books, London, March 1961, p. 238.
27. Ann Paolucci, *From Tension to Tonic: The Plays of Edward Albee* (London and Amsterdam, Southern Illinois University Press, 1972), p. 39.
28. Edward Albee, *The American Dream* New York: Coward McCann, 1961.
29. Dr. Nageswar Rao G: Preface, *Encounter with nothing* S.V. University Press, Tirupati 1979. p. 114.
30. Gerry McCarthy, *Edward Albee*, (Macmillan Publishers Ltd. 1987) pp. 115-16.
31 Michael E. Rutenberg, *Edward Albee: Playwright in Protest.* New York: Avon, 1969 p. 236.
32. Edward Albee, *Seascape* (New York: Atheneum, 1975) All Further References are to this Edition and will be Cited Parenthetically in the Text.
33. Gerry McCarthy, *Edward Albee*, (Macmillan Publishers Ltd. 1987) pp. 115-16.
34. Lucina P.Gobbard, *Albee's Seascape: An Adult Fairy Tale*, Modern Drama, Vol. 21.3 (September, 1978), pp. 307-316.
35. Harold Clurman, *Seascape - Criticism*, New Yorker, Vol. 220 (March 13, 1975), p. 314.
36. Jack Kroll, *Seascape - Criticism*, New Yorker, Vol. 85 (Feb. 10, 1975), p. 75.
37. Mathew C.Roudane, *Albee on Albee*, RE: Artes Liberales 10 (Spring 1984: 1-2 as Mentioned on Phillip C. Kollin and J Davis

Madison, eds Critical Essays on Edward Albee, (Boston, Mass: G.K.Hall & Co, 1986), p. 198.

38. *Ibid.* p. 198.

39. Edward Albee, *The Man Who Had Three Arms* (New York: Atheneum, 1987), All Further References are to this Edition and will be Cited Parenthetically in the Text.

40. Mathew C.Roudane, *Albee on Albee*, RE: Artes Liberales 10 (Spring 1984: 1-2 as Mentioned on Phillip C. Kollin and J Davis Madison, eds Critical Essays on Edward Albee, (Boston, Mass: G.K. Hall & Co, 1986), p. 190.

41. Brendin Gill, *Box & Quotations From Chairman Mao-Tse-tung*, New York, Vol. 44 (October, 12, 1969), pp. 103-104.

3

Human Relationships

A Delicate Balance

> Before they slept, they must fight; after they had fought, they would embrace. From that embrace, another life might be born. But first they must fight, as the dog fights with the vixen, in the heart of darkness, in fields of night.[1]

Man has been civilizing himself since his evolution. His aim has been to achieve the perfection of life. But it has resulted in a perverse perfection because of the technological influence. Toynbee said that man has climbed to the highest peak of civilization and therefore he either must climb down slowly or fall down to ruin. In a world beset by the scientific and technological advancement many writers and prophets agree upon marching towards the goal of universal brotherhood by various routes according to the problems that have touched their hearts. For instance, Wilfred Owen bases his 'universal brotherhood' upon the pedestal of warfare, but Albee presents his theme of human relationships on the pedestal of social welfare. To quote C.W.E. Bigsy, "To Edward Albee ...modern society has detached itself from the fundamentals and has created a new system of values by which the pursuit of material wealth and technological efficiency has come to replace basic human needs"[2] By focusing attention on the American middle class family, this chapter examines the human relationship in the family unit-between husband and wife, parent and children, and among siblings-and the debasement of values and estrangement of individuals both in family and in society.

The fundamental unit of the human community and the universal humanizing unit of all societies is the family. "A family" as defined by Ernest W. Burgers, is "a group of two or more persons, joined by ties of marriage, blood or adoption, which constitute a single household, who interact with each other in their respective familiar roles, and which creates and maintains a common culture."[3] It is indeed, the most remarkable institution wherein its members act according to the culturally prescribed roles. It is in the family, many of the most important values are learnt. The family not only transmits values, but it also symbolizes some of the distinct 'human' values: tenderness, love, concern and loyalty. The varied human relationships in the family; family struggles and disappointments, leading to social issues have been the concern of the renowned playwrights of the world.

Family, despite its disintegration in the modern age persists because of the sense of security it provides. Family life, starting from the colonial days, up to the present has been "the preferred mode of living for adults of all ages in the United States."[4] In the colonial American families, among puritans, marriage was considered a blessing. Individuals were able to find solace and comfort in their families. The family of the latter half of the nineteenth and twentieth centuries is markedly unstable, characterized by high divorce rate, lower birth rate and a smaller family size. In the modern family, which emerged as an after effect of urbanization and industrialization, emphasis was laid on social and economic values. Marital relationship was de-emphasized and money usurped the place of love.

Family considered the source of safety and security changed into a source of struggles. Absence of love and affection, lack of understanding and communication has turned most of the families into war zones. Albee exposes the American scene at the roots of the family unit. According to Albee the family is said to be breaking down and is in need of an immediate repair. Anne Paolucci comes quite close to the truth with the general assessment of Albee's works when she says "He goes beyond social commentary to the disease of contemporary life."[5] Albee more than anyone else, had the advantage of having lived through the times when the limits between old and new, known and unknown, normal and abnormal were constantly being breached. He felt gratifying to "write about imbalance within many relationships" for he has always believed that it is "imbalance, discontent" which embraces "all Drama."[6] Anita M. Stenz, in her book-length study, points out rather unambiguously that "his main areas of inquiry are failure in human relationships in whatever combinations they occur."[7]

In the first full length play Who is Afraid of Virginia Woolf? Albee portrays what American family really looks like. Albee's sharpest thrusts are aimed at the materialism, opportunism and cannibalism built into the institution of marriage. He invents the American drama of an ideal family life in order to project the reality; the real state of the American family which represents the condition of the modern society. The names of George and Martha remind one of George and Martha Washington suggesting that even the father of America had no children of his own. The barrenness of George and Martha symbolizes the barrenness of American society.

The childless couple under the strong effect of alcohol lay bare the emptiness of their marital lives. Albee has developed the theme of sterility in Who is Afraid of Virginia Woolf? Childlessness is used as a symbol of emotional sterility as in Federico Garcio Lorea's *Yerma.* George and Martha, who like Daddy and Mommy in The American Dream, feign in front of others that they are satisfied with their marriage, are aware of the failure of their marriage, which is incomplete without a child. Being discontented with "the mire of the vile, crushing marriage"[8] (P. 133) as Martha calls their marriage, they struggle against the anguish throughout their life. Both of them have accepted their struggle as an endless war. While George is "devastatingly invective" Martha is "swinishly effective" (P. 4) Despite the fact that their married life is a long, sad game, they have the unique quality of standing together for ever continuing their love-hate relationship.

In their drunken orgy, George and Martha destroy each other in brilliant dialogues of disgust and malice. They exchange verbal punches feeding on their own weakness. Words like "Braying", " Cock-spaniel", "Hyena", "Satanic-Bitch", "monster", "a spoiled self-indulgent, willful, dirty-minded, liquor-ridden ..." (P. 94) for Martha and a "simp", a "blank", a "cipher", a "sour-puss", "muck-mouth", "paunchy", "bastard", "swampy", "floozie", and "son-of-a-bitch" for George are used quite often. They attack each other with great skill and cruelty because they are afraid to face the emptiness of their lives. These epithets are a clear evidence of the opinion they have for each other. Their imaginary son fills a vacuum in their lives, but he is less a son who brings peace and comfort and more of a weapon used to attack each other for their inadequacies. The relationship between George and Martha does not improve much with their imaginary son. Both narrate the reasons for the need to invent the son and the purpose to which they interpret their fiction.

Albee has exploited the Elizabethan theme of war between the sexes. George and Martha engage in a war of sexes. Sharpening their claws they tear "through the skin, all three layers, through the muscle ... and get down to the bone," (pp. 124-125) George and Martha have tried to forget the haunting emptiness of their marriage by playing together the game of "bringing up the son" for twenty one years. The domestic warfare over shadows any hints of affection and the marriage seems to be turning from hatred to final dissolution. George by indulging in a bloodless homicide in order to subdue

Martha's pride, kills the child of fantasy in the presence of their guests, who watch them bewildered. He thus brings the secret game played for twenty-one long years to an end.

Realizing the sterility in the relationship of the older couple, Nick and Honey are forced to confess their own emptiness. Nick admits, "I wouldn't say there was any—particular passion between us; even at the beginning ...of our marriage, I mean". (P. 63) His marriage is not founded on real love and affection but on money and deception. He confesses that he married Honey because he believed her to be pregnant, whereas Honey, who tricked Nick into marriage by her 'hysterical pregnancy', secretly avoids conceiving. She is frightened by the idea of child bearing:

"No ... I don't want any ... Please" (P. 105)

The family becomes a pretense which the couples sustain by lying to themselves. They, as the couple Tobias and Agnes in A Delicate Balance do, remain within the family unit not because they are bound by mutual love and affection but because (according to Albee) "the family is the way we have devised to avoid facing the truth about our own selfish nurtures. We are alone, isolated, unable to give love but screaming to be loved."[9]

C.W.E Bigsby says that even love is counted by human beings in terms of material gains. "Therefore human relationships should exist outside the cash nexus"[10] and the society should be held together by freely acknowledged emotional and moral bonds. This is the main concern of Albee's plays. He portrays in them the pathos arising out of the loss of love in personal relationships. For example, George and Martha in Who is Afraid of Virginia Woolf? "go round the mulberry bush" for twenty –one years. They are shown at the end as left only 'with one another', with relationship. They acknowledge the responsibility which they had previously evaded; where once they had used the imaginary child as a means to accuse one another; they now accept their joint failure: "We couldn't" (have illusions anymore) As Albee himself has acknowledged there is a 'hint of communion in this'. (P. 138)

George and Martha in Who is Afraid of Virginia Woolf? destroy their symbolic family to know one another truly, but in A Delicate Balance the characters continue to use the family arrangement as a pretence to live. This play A Delicate Balance won the Pulitzer prize for Albee in 1967 and is about the 'delicate balance' which Tobias and Agnes try to maintain. In this play Albee investigates how a basic social structure, the family, is disoriented at its source. C.W.E. Bigsby observes "The play is offered both as an examination of the failure of individual commitment ... and as an account of the collapse of personal and social meaning which simply compounds a metaphysical absurdity"[11] The individual's inauthentic response towards his own life has given rise to an institutionalized monotony: "becoming a stranger in ... the world ... quite uninvolved".[12] (P. 3)

In A Delicate Balance a single family is taken for dissection. The family 'an icon of the American system' has adopted not mutual understanding and mutual dedication but mutual fear and expectation. Love, affection, and friendship are all misunderstood and misrepresented. Only the long association and the demands of the society make them live together, while everybody is a separate island by himself. Everyone has simply compromised in the battered George's style as in Who is Afraid of Virginia Woolf? "Accommodation, malleability, adjustment ... those do seem to be the order of things." This inhibits any real relationship among the members as well as towards others and everyone is emotionally estranged in their attempt to hold on and to maintain the family's shape. Family structure is there, but its harmony is lost. What Albee implies here is that the very aim of integration in the family system results in disintegration.

The setting in A Delicate Balance is the living room of a well appointed sub-urban house of the present day America.

It is a comfortable house but not a home. The family consists of six characters whose lives are hanging in a delicate balance. Tobias is the head of the family. Though he and his wife, Agnes have evolved a working relationship, they are estranged. His sister-in-law, Claire, is an alcoholic, who finds alcohol an amiable substitute for her happiness. Their only daughter, Julia "a quadruple amputee"(P. 66) and their best friends, frightened and scared; Harry and Edna, arrive one after another, seeking refuge and comfort; to a house which is already hanging precariously. Each member is forced to introspect and face his or her true image in the mirror of life.

Tobias and Agnes have been living a mechanical existence, performing to their best what ever duties are required of them for the smooth running of the house. They lead a hollow marital life, a life confined to their own shells, showing no initiative for contacting the other. Outwardly they talk amiably, calling each other sweet names and protesting what they would do without the other. There is patience and calmness on the exterior, but there is a turmoil within, which they are afraid to reveal. There is a constant tussle going on between the two sisters especially on the subject of Claire's heavy drinking which results in her misbehavior. Leading a life does not mean living the life, but protecting the titular balance. Each one seeks only self protection and isolation in a house which is devoid of love.

Albee in A Delicate Balance exposes the bleak realities of human relationships, calls attention to the failure of love and the great need for love in families. Tobias and Agnes are victims of despair of their own creation. Their house is not a home but a place where two strangers live. Tobias experiences the loss of their son at a very early age and later on he is disappointed in his love for his cat. These disappointments in love have driven him to refuse any emotional commitment and he severed all physical intimacies from Agnes, whereas Agnes suspects that her sister Claire would have been Tobias' mistress. She is further distressed and disappointed by Tobias' unwillingness for having another child. Tormented by her husband's infidelity and his refusal to commit himself both sexually and emotionally, Agnes speculates of becoming schizophrenic. Like her husband she too estranges herself from her family. Tobias has built his family not on love and affection but on alienation. The family has become the inescapable trap in which the husband and wife are caught. The failure to bridge the gap between them brings unhappiness in the family not only for both of them, but also has a grave consequence on the emotional growth of their daughter Julia.

Albee projects another angle of their family's disharmony by showing all marriages of Julia as failures. The child, who expected her parent's compassion and sympathy, is left disillusioned, because failures in her life are due to lack of understanding and communication between herself and her parents. Even at the age of thirty-six she is childish, seeking comfort from her parents, as if she is a fifteen year old girl. The home coming of their daughter Julia, once in three years after her unsuccessful marriages, reflects her parents 'unhappy married life'; wherein they never communicated with each other and were responsible for theirs daughter's precarious condition.

Eric Fromn has suggested that for many, marriage is an attempt to counter a feeling of isolation. He argues that for such people, it is "the main emphasis on finding a refuge from an otherwise unbearable sense of aloneness;" and when this fails, as it does many times for Julia, "such people continue to remain children, to hope for father or mother to come to their help when help is needed"[13] This is the reason why Julia runs to the security of her home, whenever there is a disagreement between her spouse and herself. Julia, being callow, is frightened by the external world; she seeks comfort at least in her own room. Deprived of her room, "a special room with a night light or the door ajar so you can look down the hall from the bed and see that Mommy's door is open" (P. 92) she becomes hysterical.

The loveless, tiresome relationship of the parents prevents their only child from growing. The 'delicate balance' where all are placed together, bound not by bonds of love but by blood; could never inspire the child to develop and meet the demands of the world without disillusionment.

Albee's A Delicate Balance also portrays the sibling rivalry between the two sisters. The relationship between the sisters is marred by the disgust each displays for the other. A basic jealousy marks their relationship. Agnes' suspicion that Claire could have been Tobias' mistress aggravates the enmity between them. She fears her sister to be a threat to her relationship with Tobias, and also a source of danger to the family balance. Claire who loves Tobias is jealous of her sister who is the "ruler of the roost ... and licensed wife"; (P. 149) and Agnes feels that "the one thing sharper than a serpent's tooth is a sister's ingratitude." (P. 6) Despite Claire's behavior, Agnes allows her to stay with her. It is not love, but Agnes' sympathy and patience, which allow her to tolerate Claire in her household.

Agnes by adjusting herself to all situations is able to maintain a permanent relationship with her sister. Even behind the threatening, there is the underlying care for her sister, whereas Claire, who imposes herself on others, is unable to establish any constant relationship even with her sister. She reduced her life to the world of language where she can pass sharp and racy comments about everybody. As a result she simply desires continued sanctuary from a world in which she has been crazily buffeted about.

Tobias being placed at the centre of the circle formed by family and friends, each one appealing to him for something or the other finds himself inadequate to satiate their needs; especially to Harry and Edna who have come for 'succor' and comfort'. They create more chaos in their world. Stenz explains, "Refugees from their own loneliness and loss, they come looking for the warmth and the sense of belonging which they have failed to create between themselves in their marriage".[14]

Tobias shouts and tries to tell "HARRY AND EDNA ARE OUR FRIENDS". "They are intruders" Agnes snaps back, explaining "They have brought the plague with them" and she feels that if they are not careful they may be affected "It's not Edna and Harry who have come to us –our friends – it is a disease". (P. 151) With a shattering realization Tobias asks, "… if that's all Harry and Edna mean to us, then … then what have we meant? Anything? When we touch, when we promise, and say … yes, or please … with ourselves? … have we meant, yes, but only if … if there's any condition. Agnes! Then it's … all been empty". (pp. 151-152) He could not digest that harsh truth.

Fortunately for him, Harry serves as a mirror when he confesses that if Tobias and Agnes had come to live with them, reversing the present situation; he would not take them in; they would not have the "rights", so as to impose and test their love in the name of friendship. Tobias gradually feels his way towards an understanding both of the fact of his own isolation and of the real nature of his relationship towards his friends. He finally admits that he does not love them and confesses that they are a threat to his peace of mind;

> I DON'T WANT YOU HERE!
> …
> YOU BRING YOUR TERROR AND COME IN
> HERE AND YOU LIVE WITH US!
> YOU BRING YOUR PLAGUE!
> YOU STAY WITH US!
> I DON'T WANT YOU HERE
> I DON'T LOVE YOU
> BUT BY GOD … YOU STAY!
> …
> Stay. Please? Stay? (pp. 161-162)

During this emotional crisis they undergo, Harry and Edna come close to each other and are re-acquainted. They can communicate easily with each other without feeling afraid or lonely any more.

The social and moral responsibility of an individual in society has been to preserve friendship. If friendship is to be true and lasting, it requires that "we must be helpful when we can, my dear that is the ... responsibility the double demand of friendship ... is it not?" (P. 112) Albee has created an awareness regarding the ultimate responsibility of a human being, to extend love not merely to his own kinsmen and friends, but the entire humanity as well; they believe that mankind must have faith in its own humanity and love. As acknowledged by Albee, in A Delicate Balance, "we're not a communal nation ... giving, but not sharing, outgoing, but not friendly" (P. 82) and what is lost in the contemporary society is love for humanity.

Albee has said that A Delicate Balance is essentially concerned with people who 'have not made the distinction between self and society and who have to suffer for not making the distinction'. They have discovered he insists, 'that after a certain point they have become paralyzed and can't çhange when they want to'.

Edward Albee depicts the family in its wider social setting, establishing a role for the child and completes his dramatization of the family and friends similar to that of Albee's life. Albee exploits the relationship within the family:

> To mirror the dilemma of a society, which lacks the means to build a true community, the family itself is not made a scapegoat and is not the only source of breakdown the play represents. The family is impoverished in the play; it is because Albee is exploring the bareness of a community built on a false awareness of rights. In this play the right to belong is a demand, in the way that there is a primitive desire to give affection, to create a community out of love.[15]

Edward Albee declared in 1967 that he was working on two short plays "Life" and "Death". The later, known as All Over, was performed in 1971 and the former under the title of Seascape came in 1975. Though these plays bear a certain resemblance to each other in their themes, they adopt contrasted perspectives on life. In Seascape emphasis is laid on the beginning of life and has an optimistic outlook, but in All Over we are given a picture of a life, the track of something that might have been and has its bout of melancholia, very often coupled with bitterness.

All Over is the first play in the era of the seventies and also is the first family play wherein the average age of all characters is sixty-five, except that of the son and the daughter (whose age is 52 and 45 respectively). As they unravel the sub-conscious mind, their inner self comes out. The play is about seven characters, waiting at the hospital room for the rich man-Father/Husband/lover/Best friend to die of cancer at any time. These seven characters are in search of finding out any semblance of meaning left over in their life. As the dying man breathes his last, these characters are tested and probed. Commenting on this play, Albee in one of his interviews declared:

> I write plays about how people waste their lives. The people in this play (All Over) have not lived their lives; that's what they're screaming and crying about.[16]

All Over portrays a family in the process of disintegration. This process combines with the process of dying of an eminent and affluent lawyer, who is the axis around which his whole family revolves. Now that this axis is about to be defaced, the members of the family are disturbed over the impending crisis and loss. Whether the master of the house was ill, or he had been away from his family members for the past twenty years paying occasional visits to them; makes no difference as it was not a close knit family .But still he was a tie that held the family together. Now, his death will tear the family apart. His unseen deathbed provides an opportunity for a get together among his Mistress, Wife, Son, Daughter and Best friend .Along with them are the Nurse and a Doctor and each one takes an opportunity to reflect upon the kind of life they have led.

The accent in the play All Over is upon the past and reassessment of how life has been lived. The play is more on life than on family life. Taking the family as a backdrop, Albee projects various lives which have been lives lived in various degrees of waste. Each member of the family feels, after self assessment, that he has done nothing substantial in his life except live for his own self. The wife truly remarks in the end:

> All we've done ... is think about ourselves what will become of me ... and me ... and me.[17]

Her recurrent phrase, "The little girl I was when he came to me," (P. 25) shows that she still remains the same little girl.

Albee's All Over reveals his conviction that a self-less affectionate relationship hardly exists between parents and children. The Daughter lives with a married man who will not divorce his wife. He instead gives her broken ribs and a black eye, and almost involves her family in a Mafia scandal. She tells her brother: "I feel like a child, rebellious, misunderstood and known ... so very well; sated and empty" (p. 58) She will be glad if her father dies because she can be what she chooses to be.

The son who remains a bachelor is quite immature and disappointing. He is still a small child at fifty plus and is unable to do anything substantial in life. Their mother is much relieved that neither her son nor her daughter has any child. She would prefer to end the lives when it is "... at its zenith" (P. 81) The daughter tells her brother "We'll see each other less, all of us ... will be our own affair." (P. 156) There are already signs of further disintegration in the family. The family has all gone to pieces. It is "All Over".

As Albee has shown in All Over, the failure of the siblings in establishing a warm relationship does not denote the failure of children but of their parents who have established their family on alienation and have prepared "earlier for the children to become adult strangers, instead of growing ones". (P. 131)

Though the siblings in A Delicate Balance and All Over are not bound to each other by love and compassion, something else binds them –blood and the same kind of binding exists between the husband and wife, in both the plays. As Agnes says, "... but blood binds them. Blood holds us together when we've no more ... deep affection for ourselves than others" (P. 152) Of course, "Blood is thicker than water!"

By depicting immature and psychic sons and daughters, Albee consistently reminds his American audience how succeeding generations have miserably failed to bring up children in a proper manner. Ironically, their wealth and opulence are in no way helpful to bring up morally sound children. Albee's melancholic judgment on his generation should not be viewed as "the condition of America as a nation but on the institution of the family throughout the world"[18] Albee's concern is that this erosion in the family life should be checked before it is widened and destroy the very fabric of the society.

The whole play talks about the death of the dying man but we are aware of the fact that the persons who are around him are already 'dead' in their flesh and the spirit and so they are dying a death invariably. The wife's affair with the Best Friend, the Nurse's liaison with Dr. Dey, the Mistress' illicit love with "three men and a boy" and the Daughter's life with a man "who will not divorce his wife to marry her" are ample proofs of dehumanization and deadness of spirit of the modern world. They may physically feel alive but are already spiritually dead.

Albee has opted for a family unit not because of the love or nurture it affords but because for him "family is the way that the society has devised to avoid facing the truth about her own selfish natures."[19] The family units have been preserved in all his plays despite lack of understanding, failure of love, infidelity, non-communication and alienation. In later plays of Albee, Counting the Ways and Seascape, the love-hate relationship is only between the husband and the wife and devoid of interference from others.

Counting the Ways is a random collection of skits and Albee deliberately uses the so-called formlessness just to reflect the play's subject matter, which is the state of modern marriage. Albee strongly believes that romantic love and marriage in the modern era is essentially hollow, empty and devoid of any substance and meaning. That is why he uses functional names like Mommy and Daddy, *He* and *She* too portray the modern family members.

Counting the Ways consists of modern married couple *She* and *He* who represent not a universal couple but a couple who form the core of modern American family. The couple is *She* and *He* and not *He* and *She* and therefore this family is formless. The anonymous couple is obsessed with their actions and feelings to find a semblance in their life. They define, decode and decipher in a futile attempt to establish some tangible meaning, to their relationship. In short, their whole life seems to be an affair of maintaining a 'Protocol' (*She* means both literal and figurative). *She* shouts at him

> Protocol! Protocol supersedes all things – grief, joy, all … things. We would be nowhere without it. Everything hangs on it.[20] (P. 37)

Later she clarifies her stand on it by saying that it is "the coding of orders, procedures, etiquette, formality etc", and he, in an utter disgust and frustration shouts back at her:

> Fiddlesticks! It's table of contents! (P. 39)

The loss of meaning in the couple's life is best illustrated in the play's subtitle A Vaudeville. This popular form of entertainment in the nineteenth century America suggests the atmosphere and structural qualities which Albee needed so as to reproduce the meaninglessness of the couple's lives. Their love is Vaudevillian slapstick. They mostly thrive on parody and that is what happens in Counting the Ways.

The couple in this play maneuvers each other to escape intimacy, which is the adhesive element in a family. Lack of intimacy leads them to a longing of unconscious separation. Presenting a cozy scene, they look friendly outwardly, but they are more than adversaries inwardly. They find opportunities to dig at each other. *She* wants to know whether *He* loves her, forgetting the basic principle that love is not a one-way traffic and it should be acted and not talked upon. Even if *He* says that *He* loves her, *He* may not mean it. As a man, *He* is not interested in such a question but grows suspicious of them. At the outset, they are shown "each standing on one side of the stage near their exit ways" (P. 7) which is a sure sign that they are already estranged physically and alienated emotionally. The family is not built on rock but on a sandy land.

He and *She* argue, discuss and question among themselves for clarity and understanding but there is no movement, no progress and no action as communication between them often breaks down. Once Albee said in an interview:

> There are several ways of families to hang together. One is to ask questions. Another is to ask all questions. When you ask no questions you hang together until you just disintegrate and aren't aware the disintegration is taking place and if you ask all questions you may possibly recreate a family structure but with firmer bonding.[21]

In Albee's view, one of the symptoms of the dissolution of a marriage is seen in the couple's order to be one's own self, the partners should be able to communicate but *He* and *She* have trouble with questioning and answering. Both of them do not give straight forward answers. Even at the outset, the audience is informed that all is not well with this couple.

They are both reading the newspaper. While reading the newspaper, *She* demands of him whether he loves her. *He* answers her with a monosyllabic 'Hm' and a double syllable 'Pardon' [P. 5] *She* repeats the question with an emphasis on love: Do you love me? Without giving a clear cut reply, *He* asks her why she asks him that. *She* simply wants to know,

That's all. When *He* questions her whether she wants an answer right then, *She* becomes "suddenly uncertain" (P. 6) and her waywardness is exposed. They spite each other. Children could bridge the gap but in the sterile world of Albee, this blessing is not there and even if it is there, it is either killed or mutilated. This couple is not sure of the number of their own children. *She* alternates between three or four. They are also not sure of how long they have been married. *He* says that it is seven years but she corrects him with six years but the truth is not yet come. They simply whine and grunt; whine and grunt help them heighten the strife and tension. This play is very much like Ionesco's play *The Bald Soprano,* where a married couple after a logical argument arrives at the conclusion that they must be husband and wife since they happen to share the same house, room and bed.

Scene VII, their estrangement seems to be total. *She* has placed a beautiful rose in a vase, which is a symbol of love. *He* circles it, takes it from the vase and de-petals it. This is a damaging game indeed, which *He* plays against her. After de-petalling some petals, *He* chews the rest which is otherwise killing of the remaining love between them. Only the stem is there, which means only the form or the frame of the marriage remains. As each petal adds fragrance and beauty to the rose, each emotional feeling should add to the flavor of the family life, but here *He* de-petals those feelings of love leaving the frame of life empty.

She looks at the stem. She is dismayed. She picks up the petals and relates them to the stem. She plays the game, "Me loves *He*? Not me love *He?*" (P. 17) her relating the petals to the stem is ridiculous because it is impossible, foolish and unreasonable. He actually tells this to her:

> Aren't you silly? Here's a new one,
> What were you doing? (P 18)

In other words love which is the cementing force between the husband and wife if once lost the amount of patch will be of no use. That is what exactly happens in this family. Rose, the symbol of universal love is de-petalled and chewed away by this nameless husband and the wife's relating the petals to the stem is futile and frivolous.

The physical space between the couple and their lives is a symbol of emotional vacuity in their life. He woefully regrets:

> When did it happen? When did our lovely bed ... split and become two? When did a table appear where there had been no space, in the center of our lovely bed? (P. 33)

It is common knowledge that separate beds forbid any possibility of intimacy. It chills one's heart when he deplores the two beds.

> They're not wide, those beds; they're single; They're for a solitary, or for a corpse. (P. 34)

First they escape intimacy; then separation is inevitable. There is no point of return, which leads them to the blind alley in their married life.

Her "Do you love me?" in the first scene becomes vicious and broader in the last scene. She enquires of him:

> If you love me ... how do I Know
> You love me? (P. 49)

His positive response is an eye opener to her. After giving an absolute reply to her, now He demands of her love. Her answer is dubious. She says "I don't know." But after a while, she changes her mind and assures him, "I think, I do" (P. 51) She is not sure if she loves him but she thinks that she loves him. Her cryptic words particularly the verb "think" is a specious twist of her way of life centered on sterile love. As She began so She ends the play with the same skepticism and indecision. Yet, they live a false life proclaiming to the world that they are husband and wife. As they are emotionally insensitive and spiritually bankrupt, their loss is irreparable and colossal.

Regarding the dissolution of their marriage, Albee consistently portrays a number of double images, which stand for disunity, separation and death of all sorts-namely physical, spiritual and emotional. This can be seen in the dedication of the play itself. It is for "Bill and Willy and Willy and Bill". Everything destructive seems to come in twos. This is a two-character play and a single marriage is gradually disintegrated into two. He prefers tea but she prefers coffee. She likes Crème bruise while he enjoys raspberry fool. They both narrate two stories each focusing on losses. He likes dandelions and daisies but she is fond of gardenias and roses. These images bring two things viz., "Cease and Corryton" (p.81) He bluntly resorts to the use of duality to characterize loss and destruction. While discussing his 'premature grief' [P.42] , he warns of the loss of life producing semen. He observes

"ya ... ya hard [P.43]

This is clear warning given by Albee that masturbation and homosexuality are the bare reality of American society which not only brings 'pre-mature grief' to the life but also eats away the very fibre and vitality of men whose virility is vital for a happy family.

Violating all theatrical norms, Albee has shocked his audience by presenting the emptiness of modern romantic love through the vacuity of the stagecraft and the Vaudevillian parody, the characters empty lives in the play.

Albee's A Delicate Balance, The lady from Dubuque, and Finding the Sun represent the bareness of friendship in American society. As in Who's Afraid of Virginia Woolf? and All Over, a group of people in The lady from Dubuque come together for a ritual exorcism of illusion. The appearance of sociability is quickly exposed as sham. The void at the heart of relationships is revealed. The friends meet weekly, for parties and play games to amuse themselves. They show weariness of social activities which have become compulsory in American society. As the primary character of the play, Jo asks the audience, “Don't you just hate them?”[22] (P. 6) The games are played not with interest but to spend time cheerfully among friends. As they are filled with hatred and repulsion they end up ridiculing one another ironically. The friends meet every week, as Fred says, “where else can you come in this cold world, week after week, as regular as patch work, and be guaranteed with ridicule and contempt. (P. 30) Jo's answer, “Oh! There must be lots of places, Fred. You have friends; this can't be the only place”. (P. 30) and Edgar's assurance that Fred would come to his house since he would also provide the same ridicule and contempt, discloses Albee's belief that friendship is not marked by love but by disgust.

Friendship in Albee's plays never does attempt to establish a permanent relationship among them. They have disgust for each other; and most of the times they turn out to be enemies. They accuse each other and at times torture one another both physically and mentally. No basic belief underlies their friendship; no real understanding or love binds them together. Friendship, like all other human relationship portrayed in Albee's plays is spurious. No commitment or responsibility holds them together, yet they maintain their friendship as a social ritual. Friends in Albee's plays behave like couples: “Friendship is something like marriage ... for better and for worse?”[23]

The empty games and bitter arguments, as in so many of Albee's earlier plays; are a substitute for a genuine contact. The friends in the play can display nothing beyond contempt. They fail to provide the needed comfort to Jo, Sam's wife who is dying apparently of cancer. Jo is not able to get solace either from her husband or from her friends. They except Lucinda are too terrified of her. Lucinda and Jo have known each other for a very long time and it has been Jo's habit to criticize and to jeer Lucinda when ever the opportunity strikes because she dislikes Lucinda and her ways. In spite of Jo's tyrant behavior, Lucinda shows love and compassion towards Jo.

The play like many others of Albee, is about winding down. Besides the apparent dying of Jo, there is also an extreme form of slow death of life, as it is of the disintegration of social form and the slow collapse of language. The spiritual and moral death of characters is evident through their conversation. The dying of affection, the decline of the body and the loss of political commitment are presented as parallel realities. This in fact is seen when Sam, husband of the dying Jo, speaks of his wife's decline. It simultaneously shows the collapse of the society: "Each day, each night, each moment, she becomes less and less. My arms go around ... bone? She ... diminishes. She moves away from me in ways! ... The thing we must do about loss is, hold onto the object we're losing. There's time later for ... ourselves. Hold on! ... but, to what? To bone? To air? To dust? (P. 61) As C.W.E. Bigsby says, "In one sense his (Albee) portrayal of characters in this play are what mankind has become, the play running down the curtain not only on the American dream but on the whole dream of human advancement"[24]

In society represented by Albee, the individuals remain as friends because Jo comments:

> We need surface to bounce it all of ... because it's too much trouble to change it all and because we probably do love them in spite of everything.
> (pp. 47-48)

Friends do not have anything in common among them, yet they maintain their relationship, since friendship is a necessary social commitment. Fred remarks "I am still pretending to be pleasant, but these social events are wearing out a man" (P.23) explain how parties are turned out to be indispensable in American society.

Unlike Elizabeth who seeks identity by the part he plays in Jo's life as her mother, Sam identifies himself by his belonging which is valued by his society ... both personal and material: "I'm Jo's husband, this is my house." (P. 77) He hopes to gain identity in a society which values only standards and not relations and he is left disillusioned. In a very interesting article, "Going to Hell with Albee", Jack Kroll says that all the noise about identity, death, and the end of the world may mean that Albee's living-room is really a Hi-tech Hell for the posthumous spirits of a burnt out civilization".[25] This seems an exaggeration and the living-room of Albee ... if it can be called Hell ... is a Hell in which there are Angels also in the form of Elizabeth and Oscar.

If friendship is to be true and lasting, it requires that "we must be helpful when we can ... that is the ... responsibility, the double demand of friendship ... is it not?"[26] Albee through The lady from Dubuque has created awareness regarding the ultimate responsibility of a human being, to extend love to the entire humanity. It is love that unites the human beings and the negation of it ultimately destroys life itself. According to Albee, creating a community by establishing human relationship based on love and affection has been realized as a basic need for human existence.

Albee, in bringing three generations together in Finding the Sun seems to be making one of his frequent reappraisals of the American way of life. The sense of continuity in the social set-up may or may not be there with the death of Haden representing the older generation, and with the middle generation craving only for a sense of belonging. The characters, mostly couples, unveil their hidden stories and they seem that they are able to survive only by 'finding the sun' that symbolizes life. Each character has equal genuine stories to tell and their telling and acting culminate when the sun is at the peak. The individual stories of these characters tend to converge into a common plot, which is finding the sun.

Finding the Sun is a one-act play depicting the story of two couples who decide to go on vacation together to a beach. Although, the title sounds an optimistic note, the still sad music of the culture gone away strikes a dismal note in the play where Albee for the first time openly discusses homosexuality adding to the complexity of life. By presenting tragic humor and tragic situations, Albee attempts to illustrate how a willingness to settle for a less than desirable life can lead to fear, loneliness and dissatisfaction.

Finding the Sun situates a group of people-Americans at the beach. They are all trying to find the sun-pursuing happiness as far as they are able to. There is an older couple, both of whom have lost their previous spouses. There is a mother and son named Edmee and Fergus and two sets of couples Abigail –Benjamin and Cordelia –Daniel. The two young men in the couples have previously been lovers. (A+B, C+D and B+D) Equations and triangles have to be employed to understand the complexity of modern life. It is also interesting to see that Albee for the first time opts for giving his characters proper names. They act as a formula to help us remember who is who. This is again a reminder of the universal nature of the issues faced by the individuals.

For the first time Albee dramatizes the younger generation that in his earlier plays took the back seat. All these people have come together at the beach in search of the sun; the sun illuminates everything and shows us these people as they are. We see that they are all passing their time and no one is happy. Their holiday is spoilt with deceit, insecurity and possessiveness. In the background is the relentless sea, an archetypal symbol of life as well as death. Life is perpetual flux as Charlie was forced to admit in Seascape. The characters are introduced in small family units and the families start intermingling as the action unfolds.

Benjamin and Daniel are surprised to find each other on the same beach. Abigail and Cordelia are aware that these men were lovers. Abigail would like to think that her husband is different now because he is married; besides she never lets him out of sight. But Cordelia is more down to earth and reminds her that “A leopard doesn’t change its spots”. (P. 20) Abigail’s reply is that if Cordelia has chosen to close her eyes to Daniel’s way, if they have an ‘arrangement’, then they are in a "moral quagmire"[27]. (P. 20) Cordelia talks frankly to Daniel and is probably aware of his deceits such as not admitting to see Benjamin, but she lets it be. Cordelia threatens divorce but Daniel is confident she will not proceed for the following reasons:

> You wouldn't dare! Your family'd kill you over the publicity: famous former deb, mainline family heirloom-heiress, sorry! – married to fag, file for annulment, names hubby's former hubby as ... P. 23)

Abigail just shuts her eyes to the truth and she is the one going to be hurt most by treachery.

Cordelia at least has her mother to confide in with whom she discusses the pros and cons of being married to a homosexual; But Abigail has no family to confide in. Bursting into tears she confides in Fergus whom she has met for the first time that the second tragedy in her life is being "married to a fairy!" (p. 29)

Abigail has made her life solitary one by withdrawing herself from contact and communication. She tries to drown herself, but she was stopped in time. The sun had disappeared behind the clouds while the drowning mishap took place. In all that confusion Henden had passed away peacefully in his sleep at the age of seventy. Henden's monologue in Scene Ten is about death in which he expresses humanity's fear of the real; death. He and Gertrude embody the general that produced the mixed up lot in the beach. They had managed to keep up a semblance of continuity but whether they had a sense of belonging, Henden was doubtful because he did not experience the sense of belonging though having been married to his first wife for forty-six years until she died of brain tumor. If this is the situation in Henden's generation what continuity can be expected from their children? The people on the beach appear to cling on to each other out of a sense of longing to love but not out of genuine love. The failure of relationship and love is repeated as in his earlier plays.

Albee in this play presents a variety of love-normal, homosexual and oedipal. Edmee has been clinging to her sixteen year old son Fergus ever since her husband died four years ago. They look like lovers rather than mother and son to Gertrude. Blond, handsome Fergus is the latest version of the American Dream. Fergus-whose name is linked with the trope of the sun, is in search of his own identity. He is-similar to the Young Man in The American Dream-that he is incomplete because he has never been in love with anyone. But his mother Edmee explains her identification with her son, a relationship concluding in an obsessive attachment on the part of the mother, a human connection that reflects the inversion of the mother-child relationship present in almost all dramas of Albee. Because of the excessive identification with his mother, Fergus is the most complex figure. Albee aims at "an examination of the people who have been thwarted willfully" by the social institution and "who have not created their own identities"[28]

Henden dies, but life will go on with Fergus-American Dream and hope for the future. Look! The sun's returning. What glory! What ... wonder! (p. 43)

By focusing attention on the American middle class families, the failure of human relationships in the family unit – between husband and wife, parents and children, among siblings and among friends and the debasement of values and estrangement of individuals both in family and society is shown in all the plays of Albee. He feels that the American families are estranged from the ideals and a happy family can be created only when the couple realizes the significance of 'love and mercy ... the kind you can't hold back as a reward, or use as any sort of weapon.' He says:

> When we keep something in shape we maintain its (family's) shape, -whether we are proud of that shape, or not, is another matter-we keep it from falling apart. We do not attempt the impossible. We maintain. We hold".[29]

Finally Albee says that race, religion and class become barriers to mankind and they may put men into cages when they twinkle like exhibits of creation, unable to shine everlastingly and to live happily and peacefully. Albee proposes "re-vivified human relationships as lying at the core of a reconstituted society"[30] to retain joy and peace in this world.

REFERENCES

1. Virginia Woolf, Between the acts, p. 39, Mathew Roudane, *Who's Afraid of Virginia Woolf? Toward the Marrow*, Chapter-3.
2. C.W.E. Bigsby, *A Critical Introduction to Twentieth Century American Drama*. Vol. III, (New York: Cambridge University Press), p. 249.
3. Earnest W. Burgers and Harvey Lockee, *The Family* (New York: American Book Co., 1945), p. 8.
4. Ruth Shonle Cavan, *The American Family* 3rd ed., (1963; rpt, New York: Thomas Y Growell Company, 1966) p. 3.
5. Anne Paolucci, *From Tension to Tonic: The Plays of Edward Albee* (Carbondale: Southern Illinois University Press, 1972), p. 5.
6. *A Playwright Speaks: An Interview with Edward Albee*, p. 197.
7. Anita M.Stenz, *Edward Albee: The Poet of Loss* (The Hague: Mouton, 1978), p. 3.
8. Edward Albee, *Who is Afraid of Virginia Woolf?* Great Britain: Penguin Books, 1983.
9. Tom Scanlar, *The family world of American Drama, Family, Drama and American Dreams*, p. 193.
10. C.W.E.Bigsby, *A Critical Introduction to Twentieth Century American Drama*, p. 255.
11. *Ibid*, p. 294.
12. Edward Albee, *A Delicate Balance*, New York: Atheneum, 1966.
13 Eric, Fromn, *The Art of Living* (London, 1957), p. 88.
14. Anita Maria Stenz, *Edward Albee: The Poet of Loss*, The Hague: Mouton, 1978. p. 74.
15. *Edward Albee: Tradition and Renewal,* MCMLXIX (Brussels: Centre for American Studies, 1969), p. 50.
16. New York Times (18, April, 1971) Internet.
17. Edward Albee, *All Over*. New York: Crown Publishers, 1975.

18. Harold Hobson, *Christian Science Monitor* (11 February 1972) Internet.
19. Tom Scanlar, *The Family World of American Drama, Family, Drama and American Dreams*, (p. 193)
20. Edward Albee, *Counting the Ways*, (New York: 1977)
21. Edward Albee, *Planned Wilderness: Interview, Essays and Bibliography* ed., Patricia De La Fu ente (Edinburg, Texas: Pan American University, 1980), pp. 16-17.
22. Edward Albee, *The Lady from Dubuque*, New York: Atheneum, 1977.
23. Newsweek, Feb 11, 1980, p. 57 Internet.
24. C.W.E. Bigsby, *A Critical Introduction to Twentieth Century American Drama*, Vol. III, (New York: Cambridge University Press), p. 326.
25. Phillip. C. Kolin, *Edward Albee's Counting the Ways, The Ways of Losing Heart*, Edward Albee: An Interview and Essays ed., Julian N. Wasserman (Houston, Texas: The University of St. Thomas, 1983) p. 130.
26. Edward Albee, *A Delicate Balance*, New York: Atheneum, 1966; London: Jonathan Cape, 1968. p. 112.
27. Edward Albee: *Finding the Sun*; Antaeus; Edited By Daniel Halpern, No. 66, Spring, 1991.
28. C.W.E. Bigsyby, *A Critical Introduction to Twentieth Century American Drama*, Vol. III, (New York: Cambridge University Press), p. 299.
29. Edward Albee: *A Delicate Balance*, New York: Athenuem, 1966; p. 80.
30. C.W.E. Bigsby, *A Critical Introduction to Twentieth Century American Drama*, Vol. III, (New York: Cambridge University Press), p. 260.

4

Illusion and Reality
Who's Afraid of Virginia Woolf?

> When you get down to bone, you haven't got all the way, yet. There's something inside the bone...the marrow.[1]

'Truth and Illusion' has been a major subject that has captivated the attention of many prophets and writers from the time immemorial. Man is nurturing illusions not that it is so glittering but the truth is so bitter and uncomfortable even to think of. Truth lies hidden like the marrow, the essentiality of the body structure. This illusory world serves a succor to the artists, sensitive to the pain and suffering inherent in the real world. This realization of the irrationality in the world has led many artists to create an apparently real world within his art. Fantasy remains the only compelling alternative that a poet can devise on the face of reality which is complex. As Nietzsche would say, "man is 'an incarnation of dissonance' and life to be borne needs an absorbing illusion."[2] American writers dramatized the aspect of illusion, an increasingly significant aspect of American experience which added a fresh chapter to the literature of America through the interpretation of its culture. Edward Albee takes up this recurrent theme in modern literature and deals with it in a considerable depth in his plays.

From The Zoo Story the truth and illusion is woven like a thread in all his plays but stands out clearly in these plays which have been selected in this chapter.

Illusion in European drama has been associated with the illusion of love, power, dignity or fulfillment in life. But Americans have explored a kind of illusion i.e. the illusion of success. The present America, appearing as the greatest country in the world, owing to its industrial civilization, has given its citizens, speed and plenty. To avoid being stamped 'poor' and 'stationary', it is getting used to acquire comfort and luxury but without peace and harmony. The visualization of more leisure, more income and more comfort drives them to turn out to be a prey to constant anxiety and nervousness and millions seem to fight a losing battle with this invisible enemy. Illusions of success, wealth and social recognition are the dominating features of the present American society. The highly technological civilizations of America inspired unlimited expectations of material welfare, but the promise remained largely unfulfilled for millions, for whom the dream of money-success has been reduced to an inglorious fantasy. In this fast changing world there is no place for defeat, for sorrow has to be suppressed and humiliation overlooked, though they feel frustrated and insecure in their hearts. The manufacture of illusions seems to have become a necessary activity, adding to the astounding production of wealth. They continue their battle to win with shattered hearts for 'infinite progress' and 'infinite happiness'.

Carl Gustav Jung points out in *The Plight of the Individual in Modern Society* how society has degenerated:

> Under the influence of the scientific assumptions not only the psyche but the individual man, and, indeed, all individual events suffer a leveling down and a process of blurring that distorts the picture of reality. The goal and meaning of individual life (which is the only real life) no longer lies in individual development, but in the policy of the state, which is thrust upon the individual from

> outside and consists in the execution of an abstract idea which ultimately tend to attract all life to itself. The individual is increasingly deprived of the moral decision as to how he should live his own life.[3]

Nothing has a more divisive and alienating effect upon society than this moral complacency and lack of responsibility. Their inadequate response to life is proportionate to the tenacity with which they struggle to hold on to their illusions. Claire remarks, "We submerge our truths and have our sunsets on untroubled waters."[4]

Thus a life, that is being spent outside the periphery of reality has alienated man from each other. It is somewhat significant that since 1920s the theme of success and that of loneliness have been progressively exercising the creative imagination of American playwrights. The major post-war playwrights like Ionesco, Beckett, Genet, Pinter redefined reality or rather broadened the perspective. The world of Ionesco and Beckett is founded on nihilism and absurdity. Jean Genet pointed a picture of life heavily colored with private fantasy. Almost all the modern American writers presented the culture of America in their works and criticized their own land as the greatest country only outwardly. Albee too falls in line with them. For instance, straight from his The Zoo Story he criticizes the American life, "New York ... the greatest city in the world ... Amen."[5]

The playwrights see man is wrapped up in illusions and strives to free him, so that he can see the reality of his existence. The illusion no longer serves him and it makes the world difficult to live in. A world that can no longer provide the illusion is terrifying in all its aspects. Camus voices this opinion by observing that "a world that can be explained by reasoning; however faulty is the familiar world. But in a universe that is suddenly deprived of illusions and of light, man feels a stranger."[6] The real world is juxtaposed with the illusory in order to heighten the man's dangerous position in the universe. The conflict between illusion and reality is dramatized, not in order to arrive at any conclusion but in order to heighten the absurdity of human predicament.

In a fast changing society, devoted mainly to money and material prosperity, isolation of individuals is almost inescapable. The theme of loneliness is really connected with the theme of success. "The intimacy of human relationships which is the sap of communal living, is receding at an accelerated pace and an anxious craze for status and comfort has taken the place of meaningful communicative social life."[7] In American drama, the recurring theme of loneliness for the past forty years, of men-women living lonely lives of non-recognition and denial, indicates its importance in the cultural map of the land. Albee attempts to explore the culture's reality with its unrealized dreams; the negative result of the American Dream; the 'real' which stands against the 'expected'. His dramas "reveal a harassed man, anxious for money and social status, devoid of the grace of dignity and kindliness, ready to stake anything for success, a materialist without any vision of human grandeur."[8] like Mommy in The American Dream, Peter in The Zoo Story and George in Who is Afraid of Virginia Woolf?

The theme of the conflict of illusion and reality in the plays of Albee stems from his belief that "the most moral, religious, political and social structure man has erected to illusion, have collapsed."[9] Realizing that everything in the 'slipping land' of America is not 'peachy-keen', Albee has made it his mission to make his country men; and through them the world, realize that they have substituted artificial values for real ones. Albee optimistically hopes to save mankind, by depicting the havoc that arises out of man's refusal to fall back to truths from illusion. Albee's strong conviction is that man is afraid of facing reality knowing that he rides on illusion. After having mounted upon the tiger of illusion he can neither get-along undaunted nor get down to confront it but become dumbstruck and simply sustain his fear of insecurity and instability. In all of Albee's plays, the moral implication is that everyone should be aware of one's life situation. To acquire that awareness is to rediscover reality by 'acquiring the consciousness of peril and loss and a consciousness of the 'radical crisis' present in American life in which reality has become a masquerade.' He insists that there if finally a truth to be acknowledged. Daniel Brown remarks, "His attacks are upon the deviations from some kind of implicit standard."[10] He is a stern moralist who believes that there are right values and wrong values.

Albee investigates the destructive force of the illusion ridden life through many of his plays. Albee's own comment about the play The American Dream can also be applied to his other plays: "This play is an attack on the American scene, an attack on the substitution of artificial for real values in our society, a condemnation of the complacency, cruelty, emasculation and vacuity; it is a stand against the fiction that everything in the slipping land of ours is peachy-keen."[11] Debauccer also observes, "In this work (The American Dream) he denounces, through the sacrosanct fraud of the family, the emptiness of the American life the inanity of its conformism, the idiocy of its image of success and its pseudo-culture."[12]

The American Dream is every American's vision of the future. The belief is that the present is unimportant, for it is only a step towards achievement of some ambition with full of wealth and social acceptance with fulfillment. The future of the young is assured with success and guaranteed that everything is 'peachy-keen'. The utilitarian approach however makes people become liable to ageing as to machines. Peter in The Zoo Story after having fulfilled his function as a husband and father, seeks refuge in the corner of the park bench, in The American Dream, Daddy after having fulfilled his social function in marrying Mommy and supplying her with the money she had longed to posses (while she in turn has completed her function by submitting to his sexual demands) can do nothing but moan plaintively. The failure to confront reality prevents the establishment of any meaningful relationships, and thus he cannot help being alienated from himself and from others. In their fear to face so much or reality they continue their nullified existence dispassionately, their illusory life. Even the language they speak is drained of its real meaning and thereby cliché-ridden.

The play is an account of vacuous lives and the destructive power of Mommy and Daddy. The family, an icon of the American system, is exposed as the heart of its inhumanity. Thus the parents in the play, Mommy and Daddy systematically destroy an adopted child -the new generation is destroyed in the bud. In the person of Young Man we are presented a living embodiment of the American Dream, personally attractive, totally amoral and drained of all inhumanity. The only hope resides in the figure of Grandma, an old woman who stands as a representative of older values. Mommy, Daddy, Grandma, the Young Man and Mrs. Barker-the characters in the play are the expressionistic realization of a society in which the humanizing aspects of pity, affection and love have given way to cold, clinical rationalization which substitutes commercial value for worth, and 'cool-disinterest' concern for fellowmen. Mommy is brilliant satirical comment on the product of such a society. Her most typical line is "I can get satisfaction but you can't"[13] (P. 16)

Her pragmatic philosophy is aptly shown in her 'scatter brained story of the beige-hat.' She admits that the hat she returned and the one she was given in exchange are one and the same. What matters is getting satisfaction, in being heard, in being told (by her club women) she was right, in being catered to, although everyone involved in this business including Mommy knows it is all an act. As Ronald Hayman points out, in addition to providing a comment about the way Mommy spends "her time and Daddy's money, this episode underscores her consumer attitude towards everything and everybody."[14] For Mommy, her marriage too is no more than a social contract in which she has bought wealth and security with sex:

> We were very poor, But then I married you, Daddy, and now we're very rich. I have a right to live off you because I married you, and because I used to let you on top of me and bump your uglies in" (P. 23)

Ironically, Daddy and Mommy are childless, which is a blessing in disguise, since an infant born in this atmosphere would almost be an orphan -an emotional cripple. It is highly unfortunate that Mommy bought or adopted a child from the Bye-Bye Adoption Service through Mrs. Barker, all to 'satisfy' herself. When she felt dissatisfied with the child she simply destroye 'the thing', mutilated the child as we are told by Grandma. To punish its "misbehavior", they had to put its eyes out, castrate it, because "it only had eyes for its Daddy"; cut off his hands because "it began to develop an interest in you-know-what" and finally cut its tongue out because "one day it called its Mommy a dirty name." (pp. 61-62)

Mommy is a woman obsessed with appearances and illusions. She is left with her own typical 'satisfaction' at the end when she greets and welcomes the Young Man, the 'American Dream' with delight, who is nothing but an automation, an empty shell, a prototype: "I can feel nothing ... I am ... but this you see".(P. 28) He is a fitting complement to Mommy. He has an attractive manner and is as impotent as Daddy. In fact he is the twin brother of the child Mommy had mutilated. He himself confesses out frankly : "I'm looking for work ... almost anything ... almost anything that pays. I'll do almost anything for money". (P. 72) Mommy readily accepts the illusion that he is the 'American Dream' with great joy, an extra one to her 'vociferous flaunting character' "He's very nice. Really top notch; much better than the other one. And we'll drink and celebrate. To satisfaction". (P. 91)

When Mommy asks Daddy to join in celebration, he dwindles in his usual way. His failure to confront reality prevents the establishment of a meaningful relationship with his wife. When he cuts himself off from the reality of his situation and prefers as easy 'evasion' to complex 'action' he loses his humanity and becomes absurd; all his actions become senseless, useless, and absurd. Albee directs his satire at the nullity of Daddy's life and at Daddy's false response to which he reduces. Like Peter in The Zoo Story, he is contended in alienating himself from his own self as well as from others. He has accepted his absurdity by taking part and giving approval to Mommy's petty games, to illusion herself in accordance with the society. Daddy has reached a stage where he would just like to "go away". He has failed to establish a sense of his own worth as a human being apart from his role as a good provider. "If the unauthenticated of modern life is a mark of man's desire of the human condition Albee implies that this failure of courage is not inevitable."[15] It is the culture, which warped the nature of the woman. Daddy's marriage increasingly makes him lead to live within a climate of illusion, the world of his wife. 'At any rate you are very well provided for' is all that he can say about himself, by taking into account the accumulation of material acquisitions against the missing warmth of love and relationship that might have grown between two self-realizing people.

Mommy, Daddy, Young Man, Mrs. Barker, Grandma, all are satisfied, because now Mommy and Daddy have their Young Man, the Young Man has a new house and Mrs. Barker has her adoption fee. The play ends where Grandma, assuming the part of chorus, directly addresses the audience:

> "So lets leave things — Good night dears." (p. 50)

The characters are still engrossed in their world of happiness. But the ultimate irony is that this happiness is not only false but the values which govern their happiness are also artificial. All have surrendered to a life of illusion, obsessed with the dream of success and money; everyone is blind to the real values of life. The characters are not only engrossed in the illusions of their false values but do not even pretend to have anything to do with reality. The values governing their lives are built on sand and in the opinion of Kingsley, "sand castle illusions are allowed to stand"[16]

The American Dream is a drama in allegorical form on the extent of illusion pervading American life, and the social character of this fantasy engages the playwright's exclusive attention. But Who's Afraid of Virginia Woolf? is more penetrating in its study of private face of illusion. This story of private life represents that of a thousand homes and transcends the personal and private while embracing an important aspect of the technological ethos: the need of human warmth. Martha's aggressiveness, her biting criticism of George, her careless sexual abandonment and the creation of the fictious son - all denote the deep and unfulfilled craving for human relationships. As C.W.E. Bigsby observes, Who's Afraid of Virginia Woolf? "is an elaborate metaphor for what Albee sees as a willing substitution of fantasy for reality, the destructive and dangerous infantilizing of the imagination and the moral being by fear."[17] The interaction of these ideas indicates the havoc arising out in the way of human relationships.

The play Who's Afraid of Virginia Woolf? is an exquisite piece illustrating the significance and importance of illusion in modern American life-the interaction of the external and the internal, the clash between the world of fantasy with that of reality. There is no clear cut distinction between illusion and reality in this play. The audience, along with Martha and George, lose contact with the neat distinction between reality and illusion. Martha accuses George of his inability to judge: "Truth and illusion, George; you don't know the difference", and George replies: "No, but we must carry on as though we did." (P. 119)

The play is concerned with George and Martha, and the first act has a label 'Fun and Games'. Martha's father is the president of the college and her husband might have become Head of the Department of History and ultimately her father's heir, but her husband has gone no further than an Associate Professor, and this has caused Martha to torment her husband because he has failed to live up to her expectations. After having attended a party given by Martha's father, the couple return home at 2.00 a.m. quite drunk. They seem tired more because of their life experiences than because of that odd hour. Their frustration and despair are hinted at in their gestures at the surface namely "Jesus ... H. Christ" and Shhhhh ..." (P. 10) Martha's disgust with herself and her life and her bitterness about "the whole arrangement" are all revealed in her attempt to identify herself-with laborious sarcasm. "What a cluck you are" she snaps at George to which George objects later that Martha is springing things on him all the time. There begins their quarrel, their mutual contempt, which they have been prolonging since their marriage. Their fear to alter this absurdity and face their frustrations which have made their marital relationship an utter failure and they have made it difficult to correct their errors by being alienated from each other than joining their hands to face their reality.

To aggravate George further, Martha suddenly announces that she has invited some new comers, Nick and Honey, despite the objections of George. Martha, in turn, accuses George for his failure to "do anything": "you didn't do anything; -you never do anything: you never mix, you just sit around and talk". George retorts: "What do you want me to do? Do you want me to act like you? Do you want me to go around all night braying at everybody, the way you do?" (P. 13) The younger couple-invitees of the late-night party, Nick and Honey, witness a deadly combat as their elders irritate, wound, rend and destroy one another in a horrible 'sado-masochistic game'

Martha's continuous frustration in private and public life has been leading her to seek refuge in heavy drinking, promiscuity -a series of crummy, totally pointless infidelities. Stenz says:

> ... She devoted half of her remaining energies in persecuting him (George) for not having any "personality" for being "no good at trustees' dinners (and) fund raising".

> The other half she spend drowning in self-pity for not having been able to give birth to the child she imagines would have provided her existence with meaning.[18]

She disgusts herself and says, "Awww, it's the refuge we take when the reality of the world weighs too heavy on our tiny heads ... Relax; sink into it ..." (P. 111) Instead of making her life meaningful from what is left she is still 'walking what's left of her wits'.

It is noteworthy that George is neither cruel nor sadistic but who too is frustrated and disillusioned of his expectations and thus has retreated into passive reading, an illusory world where he takes refuge. After having got his parents killed in an accident he wanted to have his life on his own terms. When George fell in love with Martha he thought that he would start his life on his own terms. But Martha's ambitions and aggressive insistence to live up to her dreams aroused in him contempt, and this jostled the whole conjugal life. Having had his ideals of a wife and life shattered he has become bookish and skeptical. If he had failed to take over or control his wife it is simply because 'there is real guilt attached to his need to be cruel.' He reminds her, "I said, here we go round the mulberry bush" (P. 94)

The disappointments, rancor, and disillusionment of Martha's married life have transformed her into a terrible gorgon from whom George has only one refuge, his books. While Martha suffers from the disillusionment of her fantasies, George suffers from his 'obsession with the mystique of success-or the appearance of it'. Martha engages herself in petty squabbling, drinking and sexual promiscuity; and George in evasion and self-delusion.

They both have become the victims of their own insufficiencies. Little by little this life of hell has diminished their hold on reality, and they have created for themselves a new world where they enact the laws, a universe of "fun and games" where they make the rules. They have also invented an imaginary child for them, to enliven their games, and have established a rule that anything about their imaginary son should be prohibited in public. They direct this life-lie as they like, recreate each instant and use it as a screen. Their escape, therefore, carries within itself not a safeguard but a destruction of self, not integrity but disintegration. When each of them, claim the child to be their own accomplice their defensive mechanism in turn becomes the divisive principle.

Martha's and George's quarrels and the games they play may or may not be suggestive of their hatred for each other. The constant humiliation of one by the other, the abuses hurled and the 'Fun and Games' are most probably done to fill the vacuum in their lives. In their effort to maintain their identity they have woven a plot, a net of illusions around their existence which outwardly permits them to live somehow or other. It is not only a defense mechanism against their own deficiencies but also against an exterior world.

However, at the end of the play George, frustrated by Martha, kills the child to correct her, to have her disillusioned. He announces the death of their 'son' before the guests, claiming to have received a telegram to that effect. He ignores Martha's plea that he breaks the "rules of the game" and continues to act as if the son and his death are real. The younger couple Nick and Honey, "the wave of the future", witness their collapse and understand that a life based on lie or fear sooner or later collapses. When they leave hand-in-hand, George and Martha are left in one another's arms, for the first time, an affirmative gesture of responsibility which they evaded before; they soberly discuss how they will there upon face a life unsupported by illusions.

The killing of the child provides a release for them from the impossible situation in which they have locked themselves into for twenty-three years. The unilateral murder of the "child", the more real illusion, is a symbolic destruction of all the illusions. The play ends where Martha as Gorgon is dying. The couple undergoes change. Crouching at George's feet, in the first rays of dawn, she pulls him tightly to her, seeking warmth and protection because now she is 'afraid of Virginia Woolf.' This is exactly what Albee wants to present -the breakdown of illusions at a critical point. The communion, which seems impossible in the beginning, is established now with both of them admitting their sterility. They come together at last, purged of all their illusions.

In a way, this revelation and the destruction of the illusion prove a boon for the younger couple as Honey, who was earlier frightened of having a child, expresses her desire to bear one. She realizes that there are also joys in the rearing of the child that compensates the sadness and pain incurred in child bearing. Though they are not offered with any solution, they are left with an opportunity to reestablish their relationship on the basis of emotional honesty, like George and Martha. The conclusion of the play nonetheless, is realistically ambiguous with George claming that "it will be better", but then quickly adding "may be" (P. 139) with it. Martha confesses being afraid of 'Virginia Woolf" but then there is a hope that with time and affection she would be brave enough to confront the truth.

In Albee's plays as in Ionesco's the recurring patterns of family and the married couple with their diverse problems is seen. Albee believes that expression of love such as 'sweet', dear, darling have lost their meaning since only hypocritical attitudes prevail in American families. He suggests that only when the couple overcomes illusion and confront with the truth of their empty life, a real relationship based on mutual love and understanding can exist between them.

The metaphysical overtones of Who's Afraid of Virginia Woolf? were clear, though muted and the model of reality was a simple amazing reality. Although George comments on the difficulty of distinguishing truth from illusion; there is finally, a truth to be acknowledged, an emotional and a factual reality. But in Albee's next original play, Tiny Alice, Albee tackled the question of the problematic status of the real more directly, addressing the nature of religious faith and the concept of spiritual truth.

Tiny Alice confused and confounded the critics and the public alike. The immediate source of the central idea for this play came in an unusual way to Albee. An idea struck him when he was reading a newspaper report of a man. Albee observed that "Tiny Alice is fairly simple, straight forward play and not at all unclear, once you approach it on its own terms. It is an examination of how much false illusion we need to get through life and also the abstraction of the deity as man needs it ... I wasn't trying to write a thesis play. It is a sort of a dream play"[19] By the time Edward Albee started to write Tiny Alice he had plenty of experience in treating the theme of illusion and reality and was in a position to develop it further, in a more subtle and complex manner. He himself described the play as:

> ... double mystery play and also a morality play about truth and illusion, the substitute images. We create ... easy virtues, easy Gods, all the Gods that we create is our own image"[20]

Julian, a young lay priest, is ordered by his Cardinal to visit the ornate gothic castle of Miss Alice, a rich and apparently old recluse who wishes to make a huge donation to the church. On his arrival, however, he is offered a salutary lesson about the nature of truth and illusion as Miss Alice throws off her disguise and appears as an attractive young woman. Julian then finds himself the focus of a conspiracy by Alice and her two assistants, Butler and Lawyer, who are apparently intent on winning him away from the church. He is asked to embrace a secular deity of whom Miss Alice is merely the surrogate. He is regarded as a suitable candidate because of his own serious doubts which had led him, on one occasion, to a mental hospital; and because, as a lay priest, he is poised-not yet committed -and may be pushed over one way or the other. In the beginning this seems to be very simple theme to deal with but in the long run it involves much more wider issue than the mere donation by the 'millionaires' lady. It is a play which like a parable is concerned about a person of spiritual integrity and his betrayal by all parties. The crisis in the pure man's life arises when; having found himself uncertain of faith, he feels normally vanished. The uncertainty stems from the loss of faith in God. The purgation of illusion becomes the theme of the play. The play deals with the corruption prevailing in the Church and as the pure one is made to succumb to the 'millionaires' naked body.

Of the five characters, in the play the Cardinal and the Lawyer hide their names. The Cardinal represents the church and the Lawyer represents the state. The Butler bears the name of a butler who is a care taker in a big a mansion. Only Julian and Alice are named. Named or unnamed they are all locked together to serve their mouse god in the mansion-model. Julian is every man. He is involved in a conflict -a conflict between reality and illusion and not a battle between virtues and vice as in the morality plays-within his soul. His innocence is unquestionable. His three experiences pivot on his confusion between illusion and reality. Julian is a victim of a kind of creation of a substitute image. We are not sure whether he is a victim of total hallucination or whether he has seen the abstraction personified. The action reveals Albee's intention to demonstrate one of his basic themes i.e. worshipping the shadow instead of the substance and resorting to materialism, greed and cruelty all in God's name will bring disaster to man.

From the beginning it becomes evident that the play is not going to be what it appears to be. The prevailing metaphor of the play ... something inside something else ... is introduced by two small Cardinals in an elaborate bird cage. Though the dialogue that ensues between the Cardinal and the Lawyer, is coarse, crude and nasty exchange, any notion that the play would be realistic, is dispelled. The threatening atmosphere created in this scene fore shadows the sinister and mysterious events to follow.

The model in the castle of Miss Alice, of which the castle is an extended replica, has a model of the model "within and within and within"[21] (P. 26). This Chinese box idea of something small inside some thing large is constantly alluded in the play, and is reinforced visually by the almost continuous presence of the model on the stage. The emerging of Miss Alice as a young and beautiful woman from her disguise of a "withered crone" (P. 48) with gray hair, establishes the basic theme of illusion and reality. It becomes evident that the things are not what they appear to be in the castle. This illusion is broken at this stage and Julian, recovering his composure, discloses the secret of the six missing years in his life, when he was in asylum, to his Miss Alice.

Julian narrates the experiences he had during his stay in the asylum, where there is again an evidence of confusion between illusion and reality. Julian cannot say for sure whether his experience with the woman in the asylum was purely imaginary or real. Whatever he relates may be sheer fantasy rather then delighted consummation. He is uncertain whether 'this thing happened or ... it did not happen" and also when it happened, "at noon or in the morning, much less at night" (P. 61) was there a woman such as he describes who claimed to be the Virgin Mary? Did he actually experience a union with her and did she really become pregnant with "son of God" as a consequence. Julian doesn't have a definite answer to these questions and he cannot say whether the "... memory of something having happened (is) the same as it having happened?" (p. 65)

Julian has to be stripped off his world of illusions and be made to accept truth. The Lawyer, the Butler and Miss Alice take upon themselves the duty to bring him back to reality. Miss Alice, by her womanly charms, would entice Julian, the celibate into embracing physically and symbolically something other than an indefinable sense of God. Julian is to be sacrificed for his faith to an abstraction in exchange of the benefit of two billion dollars given to the church by Miss Alice. Julian who:

> ... is walking on the edge of abyss, but is balancing can be pushed ... over, back to the asylums rover ... to the Truth. (p. 106)

Miss Alice is Alice's image and Julian is supposed to accept the abstraction. The Lawyer tells him:

> There is an abstraction, Julian, but it cannot be understood. You cannot worship it ... There is Alice ... That can be understood. Only the mouse in the model. Just that ... The Mouse. Believe it. Don't personify the abstraction ... limit it, demean it. Only the mouse, the toy. And that does not exist ... but is all that can be worshipped ... accept it. (P. 107)

Miss Alice succeeds in seducing Julian and making him marry her. Julian does not realize that there are two different Alice's, the Miss Alice who forsakes him and the Tiny Alice whom he has loved through the former. In reality only Miss Alice exists and Julian confuses her with the image of Alice the model. Miss Alice can only provide him with temporary physical and mental gratification. Unable to understand this, Julian thinks he has entered into a permanent relationship with her. But his illusions are shattered when Miss Alice desperately begs him:

> ... have done with forgery, Julian; accept what's real. I am the ... illusion. (p. 167)

Unlike the Lawyer, Julian has not earned "never to confuse the representatives of a ... thing with the thing itself", (p. 39) instead, he invests an untrue reality. He thinks it is God's plan for him to marry Alice and mistakenly establishes her as his new deity. Not realizing that the two, God and Alice, are separate, he worships the latter in the form of former. Resisting the Lawyer's command of accepting abstraction, Julian brings upon himself the punishment planned for him: death. After much debating and questioning, Julian is compelled to accept Alice. A great shadow fills the stage and the presence of Alice is felt in the room. With her arms open wide in a crucified fashion, Julian accepts Alice and cries out "I accept thee, Alice, for thou art come to me. God. Alice ... I accept thy will." (P. 190) As he accepts God/Alice, as he abandons the need for symbols, a sense of calm prevails over him and he dies sainted. He finally accepts Alice, the abstraction, a quality, an essence which must be sensed, believed in, but never mistaken for any thing substantial or real.

The play urges us to stop using religion as armor to protect ourselves from the abstraction which is God. Since it is difficult to define the meaning of God, Julian has choice before him; to remain alive and serve Alice, or to return to asylum or to die. He chooses death and embraces Alice, the symbol of God created by man. The tragedy of Julian lies in the fact that he, who withdrew to the asylum precisely because he found himself "dedicated to the reality of things, rather than their appearance" (P. 138) still proven incapable of seeing through the symbol, incapable of realizing that in accepting Miss Alice he is not accepting reality but the mage, a seductive and attractive image of that reality. This is an illusion and Miss Alice is a "surrogate priestess" for the Tiny Alice that lives within a tiny world of truth. Julian is sacrificed, not as he expects and wants to, to a real cause, a real God, but to the image of the God and at the end ironically, is forced to admit that what he had been working for all this while was illusion.

In Tiny Alice, Edward Albee has tackled the question of the problematic status of the real more directly, addressing the nature of religious faith and the concept of spiritual truth. An explanation of the text is to be found in Edward Albee's papers at the New York Public Library:

> It will be revealed by Julian ... that Miss Alice is surrogate for the woman Julian thinks she is; that the true Alice, if indeed, she exists at all ... exists in the model, and that they must act on what they assume to be her wishes. When Julian is forsaken by others, after-being shot at, he "begins a semi-hallucinated monologue, half to God, half to true Alice ... if she exists, if in fact, there is a difference between her existence or non-existence and between her identity and God's ... Julian dies, accepting the existence, accepting the crucifixion"[22]

Like Tiny Alice, Three Tall Women is a puzzle but with a difference -instead of the mansion with Miss Alice and the model with the mouse, there are three tall women. Albee draws the audience into two worlds in this play -the totally naturalistic world of Act One, whose three tall women are a law clerk - *C* who "looks rather as *B* would have at 26", a ninety-year old mother- *A,* being a wealthy, "very old woman, thin, autocratic, proud as together as the ravages of time will allow" and her nurse - *B*, we are told "looks rather as *A* would have at 52",[23] (P. 1) or the presentational-staged world of Act Two where a maternal, mystical identity falls to each actress. They are three separate women and are inter-changeable. Divided into two acts, the first act takes place while *A* is physically present, and the second after her virtual death.

In the present time, *B* and *C* are employed by *A*. *B* is obviously the nurse as she looks after *A*'s physical need and uses scientific terms to refer to *A*'s habit of wetting:

> In the morning, when she wakes up she wets -a kind of greeting to the day, I suppose: the sphincter and the cortex not in sync. Never during the night, but as she wakes. (p. 12)

She is also detached and clinical in her attitude and rather "cruel" at times, very much like Butler in Tiny Alice. *C* is a Lawyer's representative and has come to get some of the *A*'s lapses seen to.

Although, to begin with, they are different women, in Act II they can identify with one another. It turns out that *C*, who is only 26 and is the youngest needs to be educated by *B*, who is twice her age and *B* and *C* can learn a lot from *A*, the oldest whose age is not mentioned, but who must be twice the age of *B*, because *B* 'looks rather as *A* would have at 52'. Why don't we learn from the mistakes, Albee seems to be asking through this play. On one level the play is memory from a different level of consciousness. *A* looks back at her life and sees the mistakes, which is why *C*, the youngest character keeps repeating again with reference to *A* and *B* and that she will not become like them. If *A* is nearly 100 years old, the story of mankind hasn't changed for more than a century. It is only by looking back that Albee can give the audience a perspective and urge them not to repeat the patterns of the past -the patterns of illusion rather than truth which are recurrent from one generation to the next.

There are three generations in Three Tall Women, where Albee examines the nature of illusion from a different perspective, mutation of consciousness or the interchangeability of persona. The equation here is: *A=B=C.* If individuals are subject to flux, then it follows that the notion of truth too is subject to change. The Three Tall Women seems to be having three tall tales.

Act I is basically *A's* story. Albee's strong composite heroine, *A* with a prodigal son, divulges her prejudices, her attitudes and insights on the lack of substance in the upper crust into which she was married. The two other on stage characters, *B* and *C*, materializations of her self before childbirth and at middle age, hear the older component bemoan her husband's and friend's 'lack of back bone or moral fiber'. Regrettably, her disillusion has led her to replace the legendary milkman or back seat of a car with the family's groom or stable.

Her first lessons in life were taught to her by her mother because "... we were girls and that was way back then, and it was different then". (P. 20) She and her sister were properly brought up by their mother. As *A* puts "... she tried to prepare us ... for going out in the world, for men, for making our own way" (P. 20) *A* succeeded in finding a man who had already been married twice. Her sister did not marry until she was almost forty and they had to get someone for her. She was reluctantly made to marry "a wop, whatever that meant." (P. 45)

The man *A* married was short, loved riding and kept horses. They were famous, had a famous stable and won almost all the prizes. While *A* narrates *B* is able to empathize especially when she recollects things about a bygone era. *C* can only smirk and listen in disbelief, so far removed in time is she. *A*'s son who also belongs to the same generation as *C* does not like the way she talks but for her prejudiced remarks regarding Jews, Wops, Niggers, etc., come naturally and she does not find anything wrong in it. She goes on to describe her husband, while *B* and *C* listen to her without much involvement. *A* always had her "eye out" and she was strong so she was hated by everyone-her mother, her sister and even her son who ran away from home: "Because I was strong, I was tall and I was strong" (P. 60) *A*'s story as related by her reveals "the long unpleasant life she led" while keeping her memory clearly alive with the happiness, deceits and losses especially the death of her husband and the son who got away.

Act I paints the landscape of *A*'s old age-the humiliations of incontinence, memory loss, confusion and regret "I've shrunk!" she says over-whelmed by confusions, real and imagined, that beset her. "I'm not tall! I used to be so tall! Why have I shrunk?" (P. 46) She growls, squawks, rages through the torrent of emotions and memory that's called out of her by *B* and *C*. *A*'s life turns out to have been a series of punishing losses:'a sister who became drunk; a mother who, when moved into her daughter's home, became her enemy, a son who became a stranger; a husband who became first a philanderer and then a victim of cancer.'

When Act II begins, a dummy of *A*, is propped up in be with an exact life mask of the actress playing A, although the virtual death of *A* is signified by dummy, she goes on living, as she will in the form of many *A*'s to take her place. She is irreplaceable but she is interchangeable. *A* says, "I was going to, but then I forgot, or it slipped my mind, or something. ... "(P. 68) The moment is electrifying. The body in the bed turns out to be mannequin. Albee from familiar external reality takes us into bold interior one through *B* and *C*, who are the projections of *A*. So, while A is dead and alive at the same time, it is time for the 'education' of *C* as it was for Julian in Tiny Alice. *C* cannot yet face the prospect of ageing or dying as is evident in several of her reactions even in Act I. *C* at one point in Act II points to *A*, the dummy with rage and exclaims: "I will not become ... that!" (P. 69)

But as *B* begins talking about her life, which is what Act II is partly about, it can be seen that it is very much like the one we have heard of in *A*'s life-in fact; she echoes several incidents from *A*'s life. The physical resemblances too are there-she is tall and striking. She too had a mother who was: strict but fair, like *A*'s mother and wanted the best for herself and her sister. She too has her "eye out" for the man of her dreams but has had a few flings meanwhile. The thought of infidelity put her off from marrying: "Why should I marry him, if I'm down; adjust; settle in: Men cheat; men cheat a lot, we cheat less, and we cheat because we're lonely; men cheat because they're men" (P. 82) All three share the same history, the same child, the same sexual experiences, but *A* and *B* are united against *C* in their hatred of illusions. They warn *C* that her future will be one of deception and infidelity. *A* has something to say about this and it is a page taken out from her own experiences:

> No, we cheat because we're bored, sometimes. we cheat to get back; we cheat because we don't know any better; we cheat because we're whores. We cheat for lots of reasons. Men cheat for only one -as you say, because they're men. (pp. 82-83)

A's whole story is not heard from *A* itself, *B* has changed into *A* so easily that she is the one who, in a long narrative, reconstructs the patches in *A*'s life that were only hinted at in Act I. Although *C* says she has had enough, the other two will not leave her alone unless she had been educated about death too as signified by dummy of *A* propped up in bed.

A now proceeds with the lesson on death. She is dead but it is her consciousness that is present on the stage and talks to her son about how she died in the hospital.

> ... In my premonition I knew I was dead, and it didn't seem to matter any, and I was all alone. There was no one there with me and I was dead! No one! Just the Chauffer and the maid. I was there an hour, and I was dead and then you came in, and you had flowers, your freesia. You came into the room, and they were there, and I was dead, and you stopped at the door of the room and you knew the right away and you stopped and you ... you walked over to the bed, and you touched my hand, and you bent down, and you kissed me on the forehead ... for them! They were there and they were watching and you kissed me for them! (P. 106)

Would *A*'s sorrow have been mitigated at the sight of her son weeping? Time happens too late for him now that she is on a different place, altogether totally detached from the world of senses: "I'm here and I deny you all" (P. 107) The final renunciation is addressed in general to all including the audience. But she challenges her listeners to "deny" her (death) in the sense of refusing to accept the only reality. So the word deny is used in two subtly different senses of renunciation and rejection. After a painful search for serenity with the materialized components of her selves, *A*-the ultimate mother-image realizes that the joy lies not in the events of our lives but in surcease when each of her conflicts ends. Alone, at the mercy of caregiver's and her own infirmities, she rejoices in the surcease of anxiety over real or imagined results of her actions or misjudgments of the past.

C will not accept rejection and death as inevitable and it makes her reiterate without anger though: "I ... will ... not ... become you. I will not. I ... I deny you. (P. 107) She is only 26 and hasn't had her share of happiness the 'happiest moments she begs for confirmations from her experienced sisters: "... I know my best times ... please". (P. 107) *B* can reply that at fifty she is at the peak of the mountain, at a vantage point with a 360º view. She is not going to let herself be put down by "decline", "obsolescence" or "peculiarity". Like her counterparts, Nancy in Seascape and Gestrude in Finding the Sun, she is going to join whatever is left of life. Of course, *A* who has gone to the other side and attaining the end is the happiest moment, "when it's all done. When can we stop? When we can stop". (P.110) Albee in this play has stripped away bourgeois illusion and has progressed steadily from the reality of illusion to the reality of reality. He has left to the audience to choose between chimeras or the ultimate truth.

Albee has described Three Tall Women as an "exorcism", the original title of Who's Afraid of Virginia Woof? What gets exorcised -killed off-in Woolf is the imaginary kid. In Three Tall Women, the kid kills off the memory of his mom. As in previous plays, the author is more concerned with the characters and situations than with problems and their resolutions. Albee's power to generate real characters is legendary; and his delicate drawing of this newest one, a tall mother, whose indiscretions alienate her son, brings out the turbulent relationship with her homosexual son. Three Tall Women bears witness to the son's sad wish to be loved, but with this liberating difference: the child is now finally in control of the parent's destiny instead of the parent's being in control of the child's.

Albee through this play warns that in a land where populace is obsessed with self-fulfillment and determined to be happy, "what must cease at once is our perpetuation of our offspring's notions that in life we get what we want, that parents and the world at large are perfect caregivers - or even caregivers at all."[24] Albee feels that mothers must prepare the world's young for the actualities of a life in which "surcease or a series of surceases" is out only joy. He says "Truth is out only salvation. So long as we hide from our children the sad truth of our imperfections and our mutability, we must expect the tragic splits that rend mothers and children."[25] Albee moves from his demons towards joy, surcease, and death; instead of disillusion.

Albee's particular subjects recur in his writings-the most obvious one here being the presence and absence of the baby, which has famous precedent in Who's Afraid of Virginia Woolf?

(Which also features a baby of questionable reality) and A Delicate Balance (which also features a mysterious couple.) The issue of genuine or misplaced faith is repeated in The Play about the Baby. The Play about the Baby is Albee in Vaudeville mode. The characters-Man, Woman, Boy and Girl - inhabit a timeless space where they engage in games of love, loss, pain and memory. In the first act, Boy says, "Our reality is determined by our need,"[26] which is then illustrated as the Boy and the Girl eventually face a reality determined by their need to believe in an imagined rather than a real child.

The question of illusions is central to Albee's absurd philosophy of life, and is revealed in this chamber play, The Play about the Baby. Like Who's Afraid of Virginia Woolf?, baby pits the young, naïve couple, Boy and Girl against the older couple Man and Woman. As for the play, it is more than anything a nod from Albee himself to all themes: "games playing that toys with cruelty ... reality pitted against illusions ... humor that is shadowed by a sense of doom ... macabre events ... characters whose motivations are never neatly parsed but whose words can be brilliantly playful ... heterosexual passion mixed with intimations of homoeroticism."[27] The plot centers on a baby whose existence is 'to say the least, problematic.'

The play opens onto an abstract expressionist Eden with lovely, handsome couple-barefoot and lightly dressed-sitting in a pastel nursery amidst giant-sized alphabet blocks and a monument sized pacifier, with a rocking horse and a pram suspended dreamlike above their heads. They are named as Girl and a young Adonis named as Boy are passionately in love with each other. They chat, cuddle and flirt to no end. They flaunt their casual sexuality to each other. The Girl goes off briefly to give birth, and quick as a wink she's carrying the new born in a blanket with a flashing self-congratulatory grin. The Girl's periodic feedings seem like only breaks from her constant love-making. Delighted with their achievement and treating parenthood as no-problem perk, the two are thrilled with the new born baby and again start their life of romping naked around nursery, tickling and teasing each other like two puppies and make remarks like, "I'm hard all the time".(P. 24) These young playmates believe they have reinvented the world in their own likeness.

Into the midst of the Boy and Girl's narcissistic leisure stroll, as if they were Adam and Eve in early-days, trying out for few sexual experiments, until the serpent, or rather serpents, intrude into the happy young couple-the Man and the Woman. They are dressed with a comfortable upper-class elegance that matches the casual grace of their voices and gestures, this sophisticated older couple might be the grand parents, but their relationship to the young couple turns out to be far more mysterious. The Man and The Woman are charming, witty, intelligent storytellers and tell stories as if to convey humbly that they're not just vindictive symbols of metaphysical truth. The Woman gets a long, comically overwrought description of her youthful love affair with a famous painter, which sounds cribbed from somebody's memoir. She juggles her breasts at whomever she nears. The Man's anecdotes, in contrast, tend toward Vaudeville-routine nonsense, like the one about his children, being black, white and green (Half green? Pale green) He seems like a skeptical type, and styles the play's action as his dirty experiment "What's true and what isn't," he pretends, "is a tricky business, isn't it?"(P. 37) The elders take immense pleasure in frightening and punishing the naïve young narcissists, but do so with a bag of tricks. Speaking as the voice of experience, the older couple sets out to convince the youngsters that the baby never existed in the first place. What's true and what isn't turns out to be a tricky business indeed.

The Play about the Baby weaves back and forth through the characters imagined lives. The focus on the young couple's Eden-like beginning is quickly shifted to the authoritative cynicism of their elders. There are many lessons taught by Man and Woman whose unwitting and unwilling pupils are of course Boy and Girl about life. A child has been born. Innocence is over. The play progresses in a self-conscious fashion as the characters take turns addressing the audience and flamboyantly characterizing themselves through anecdotes. More than once, Man asks of the cast, and, indeed, of us, "If you have no wounds how can you know if you're alive? If you have no scar how do you know who you are? Have been? Can ever be?" (P. 50) And later, "No, we wouldn't break your arm. Your heart, though; we would break that." (P. 50)

This play reminds of Who's Afraid of Virginia Woolf? in which the older couple George and Martha initiates a younger couple Nick and Honey into the unseemly games people play. However Man and Woman might be George and Martha who have left their home New Cathrage and are now wandering around dispensing their hard-earned wisdom. The game played is also about a baby whose very existence becomes a matter of debate. And these plays are firmly agreed upon that truth and illusion, as Martha was, are mutable and interchangeable. Man speaks sharply about truth and illusion 'Pay attention to this. What's true and what isn't is a trick business, no?' But while George and Martha worked hard to convince Nick and Honey of the existence of a fictional child, the Man and Woman in this play spirit away the title infant and then try to persuade the Boy and the Girl that there never was such a thing. Like Albee's other works, the play is a mind game, but also, like his other works, we are unsure just whose minds are being played with. Ultimately, the older couple departs, but by then we have begun to wonder what has been lost, by whom, and why and we are unsure of what was reality or not.

The Baby is real even if it is not made visible because Girl has given birth to it. In an interview Albee affirms the child's existence: "We see its blanket. She's nursing a blanket. She's not crazy. And she has mother's mild, so obviously she's had a baby"[28] What seems to be reality for a character is absurd for an other, unless the absurd turns real. Woman and Man turn real into absurd and steal the baby of Girl and Boy, a deed they deny by negating the very existence of the Baby.

The baby constitutes the dramatic blind spot of the play and is the homograph character that encodes both the issues of birth (baby) and adoption (nothing)

Girl: WHERE IS THE BABY?! WHAT HAVE YOU DONE WITH THE BABY?

Man: What Baby? (Silence)

Woman: Yes, what Baby (P. 28)

The play is a disturbing account 'about life'. Life for the young characters is reality, as they perceive it in their bodies. However as Albee claims 'reality is determined by one's need' and therefore Girl and Boy 'realize they cannot take the pain and loss of having a baby, so it ceases to be real.' The final touch of the child's mystery is provided by Man, the wizard figure of the play who decides about the existence of the Baby like George. Man says:

> Ladies and Gentlemen! See what we have here! The baby bundle! The old bundle of Baby! (*throws it up in the air, catches it, Girl screams)* (...) (*To Boy and Girl)* I know what I'm doing ... The old baby bundle ... treasure of treasures, light of our lives, purpose-they say-of all the fucking, all the ... well, all the everything. Now the really good part, the part we've all been waiting for! (*He takes the bundle, snaps it open, displays both sides, we there is nothing there)* (...) You see? Nothing! No baby! Nothing! (*Girl goes to blanket, Man gives it to her, she searches it, cuddle it, weeps. To Girl)* You see? Nothing (P. 48)

In The Play about the Baby, Albee manages to transform the exorcism of the two young characters, reality into absurdity, in a burlesque battle over a baby whose gender remains a secret. Is the Baby real because the young couple says so or unreal because the older couple says not? Perhaps Boy and Girl don't know themselves, or each other, as well as they might, though they romp around in nude often enough to have a thorough acquaintance with each others physical surface. It is exactly like 'real' life, where we don't spend our time thinking about meaning of being. Woman and Man decide that the "brave and wise" (P. 50) Girl has no Baby. They advise the young to learn from "wounds"(P. 50) Boy finally acknowledges, while the elder one leaves the stage and the play ends in a denial of the Girl's and Boy's baby in an atmosphere of almost tragic sacrifice. However, Girl hopes to have another baby, "maybe later" when they "are older" (P. 50)

The plot of this drama might suggest-beside the game of illusion and reality-a possible adoption that happens after the baby's kidnapping. In this sense The Play about the Baby echoes the theme of adoption-as a baby-by the Albee couple. The figure of the baby is real and fictional at the same time like that of an adopted child with unclear origins. In talking about the fictional son George and Martha in Who's Afraid of Virginia Woolf? says that 'fantasy child can be just as real as any real child' and, indeed this is the issue also in The Play about the Baby, Albee's other play on the exorcism of the child figure.

Tom Jones and Harvey Schmidt declared more clearly and briefly 'Without a hurt the heart is hollow,' in their *The Fantasticks,* 40 years ago. Albee, by declaring about faith, truth and illusion, and the conviction with scars that awaken us to life, shows through his art to rectify or avenge wrongs done. It is a common knowledge that he was abandoned by his natural parents and adopted by a couple, chilly to the notion of parenting and through his The Play about the Baby critics could say that, with Boy and Girl, he gets to punish his biological parents, and with Man and Women, he gets to expose his adoptive mother and father as lubricious and treacherous. More to the point, it is an allegory about the elusive and absurd nature of truth and memories.

In use of illusions, Edward Albee is unlike the European absurdists who regard absurdity as metaphysical reality. For Albee, man's absurdity is of his own creation. If his characters create illusions it is because of their failure to face the horror of their metaphysical situation. Edward Albee urges that the confrontation of reality is an aspect of man's dignity. To Albee illusion becomes an escape from guilt as Julian in Tiny Alice. The characters in Albee's plays cling on as long as they can to their illusions, willing to sacrifice their freedom, but Albee forces them to confront reality and in turn give meaning and dignity to their lives.

The action of Albee's plays often dramatizes the process of the collapse of illusion which brings the audience face to face with reality that is hidden behind the illusions. Ruby Cohn says:

> Albee has tried to dramatize the reality of man's condition, but whereas Sartre, Camus, Beckett, Genet, Ionesco and Pinter present that reality in all its logical absurdity, Albee has been preoccupied with illusion that screens man from reality.[29]

This reality that lies right behind illusions is brought to the forefront in a climax of the play and the protagonists have no option but to face it.

Albee introduces illusions in his works "only to reassess it, to show how his characters must rid themselves of falsehood and return to the world in which they must live."[30] His characters after all, are only human beings inclined towards moments of weakness, but in the end they emerge as winners and confront truth with courage and fortitude. Through the treatment of the theme of illusion and reality, Edward Albee shows the people the absurdity of the human condition, makes them aware that illusions are dangerous; that a life lived with illusions is a false life and can bring about permanent harm to them. All Albee protagonists are urged to assess their life condition, look for causes of disharmony, imbalance, isolation and unhappiness and make efforts to remove them. According to him the wall of illusions that man builds around himself is the root cause of unhappiness and unless he breaks this wall he cannot achieve happiness and peace.

REFERENCES

1. Edward Albee, *Who is Afraid of Virginia Woolf?* (Great Britain: Penguin Books,1983) p. 125.
2. Nietzsche as Quoted by Lawrence Kingsley, *Reality and Illusion: Continuity of a Theme in Albee*, Educational Theatre Journal, 25 1 (March 1973), p. 71-72.
3. Carl Gustav Jung, *The Undiscovered Self*, Trans. R.F.C.Hall (New York, 1957) pp. 21-22.
4. Edward Albee: *A Delicate Balance*, (New York: Athenaeum, 1966) p. 93.
5. Edward Albee: *The Zoo Story*, (New York: Coward, McCann and Geoghegan Contemporary Drama, inc., 1959) p. 45.
6. Albert Camus, *The Myth of Sisyphus*, tr. Justin O'Brien (London: Hamish Hamilton, 1960), p. 13.
7. A.D. Choudari, *The Face of Illusion in American Drama*, (Delhi: Macmillan Company, 1972), p. 38.
8. *Ibid*., p. 6.
9. Edward Albee, *Which Theatre is the Absurd one*? The Modern American Theatre, ed. Alvin Kernan (New Jersey: Prentice Hall, 1967), p. 172).
10. Daniel Brown, *Albee's Tagets*. Satire News Letter, (Spring 1969), p. 47.
11. Edward Albee, Preface, *The American Dream* (New York: Coward-McCann, Inc, 1967), p. 8.
12. Gilbert Debauccer, *Edward Albee: Tradition and Renewal*, Trans. A.D Williams (Brussels: American Studies Centre, 1967) p. 37.
13. Edward Albee, *The American Dream*; (New York: Coward, Mc Cann, 1960).
14. Ronald Hayman, Edward Albee (London: Heinemann Educational Books Ltd., 1971), p. 29.
15. C.W.E. Bigsby, *A Confrontation and Commitment: A Study of Contemporary American Drama* (London, 1967) p. 79.
16. Lawrence Kingsley, *Reality and Illusions, Continuity of a Theme in Albee*, Educational Theatre Journal, 25, (1 March, 1973), p. 73.
17. C.W.E. Bigsby, *A Critical Introduction to Twentieth Century American Drama*, (NJ: Prentice Hall, 1975) p. 265.

18. Anita Maria Stenz, *Edward Albee: The Poet of Loss*, (The Hague: Mouton, 1978) p. 44.
19. Interview on 22nd March 1965, at Billy Rose Theatre, New York.
20. Newsweek, Jan. 4, 1965.
21. Edward Albee: *Tiny Alice* (New York: Athenuem 1965).
22. C.W.E. Bigsby, *A Critical Introduction to Twentieth Century Drama, Vol II*, (Cambridge: Cambridge University Press, 1984), pp. 280-281.
23. Edward Albee, *Three Tall Women*, Penguin Books, U.S.A. Inc.
24. Jeane Luere, *A Review from Three Tall Women*, Theatre Journal, Vol. 44, No. 2, May 1922, pp. 251-252, as qtd in Contemporary Literary Criticism, Vol. 86, p. 118.
25. *Ibid.* p. 118.
26. Edward Albee, *The Play About the Baby*, New York: Dramatists Play Service, 2002.
27. Mel Gussow, *A Singular Journey Begins*, p. 397, (Online, Internet).
28. *Ibid.*, p. 398.
29. Ruby Cohn, *New American Dramatists*, (London: Macmillan, 1982), p. 5.
30. Diana Trilling, *The Riddle of Who's Afraid of Virginia Woolf?*, in Edward Albee, ed. C.W.E.Bigsby (Englewood Cliffs, N.J., 1975), p. 87.

5
Alienation
Finding the Sun

Alone, alone, all, all alone;
Alone on a wide, wide sea.[1]

The Ancient Mariner suffered from a sense of aloneness on a "wide, wide sea": guilt-haunted, tortured in spirit, he was a lone voyager on a vast sea of life. Cut off from the roots of life and torn from the centre of creative love and fellow-feeling, man lives the life of a stuffed creature, trying to maintain a delicate balance between appearance and reality, and struggle to maintain the balance in an extremely painful one. Alienation can be found in literature from Beowulf to the modern fiction of today. Alienation is one of the major themes that render a great concern in America and Albee handles the theme of alienation in his plays in a variant form which is taken for study in this chapter.

Alienation has been one of the major factors contributing to the painful and embarrassing agony that man has been undergoing since his creation. God gave life to man but man chose death for himself. Even the Bible has treated this theme of alienation-Eve fell alienating herself from Adam who in turn fell, alienating himself from God.

Alienation both as a human experience and a subject of literature is not an exclusively Twentieth Century phenomenon. T.S. Eliot's *The Waste Land* published in 1922 distressingly projects the loss of traditional values in the European society which alienated man from both God and his fellow-men. To Eliot alienation from such strong and secure roots made man a hollow creature. *The Waste Land* is a record of their alienation, and it suggests through a recall of myths, how such alienation can be fought by man and how certain creative values can be built in a disintegrating society.

Modern society with its set norms and codes of behavior and with its conditions for success and fame is one of the most prominent causes for the increase of alienation in individuals. Murray Levin says "the essential characteristic of the alienated man is his belief that he is not able to fulfill what he believes in his rightful role in society."[2] All alienated characters are themselves not responsible for their condition. Most of the times it is the society that is the 'villain'. The advanced mechanized society with its machines and other artificial creations creates a barrier which results in the loss of self-identity.

Since drama is an important aesthetic medium for reflection of life, it is not strange that major dramatists are concerned with these problems of alienation and loneliness in their works of art. The presentation of the themes of loneliness, rejection, alienation is a recurrent feature of present day literature as it is of present day life. Antidotes to alienation frequently used in daily life by many alienated characters and perhaps suggested by many writers themselves are-copulation, use of drugs and intoxicants. Whether they really help them is uncertain. The irony of it all is that the writers themselves are unable to ward off alienating circumstances. It is interesting to note that the best writers are alienated men writing about the alienated heroes in an alienated society.

The 'themes of alienation' perhaps began without its absurdist overtones, but with the 'problem' Playwrights in

England, such as Galsworthy and Shaw in whose plays we find various preoccupations with certain problems of society where individuals are alienated not only from the society but also from the true essence of their own life. Such expressions, in a way are an immediate outcome of economic and political injustice prevailing in the society. In the field of poetry, the theme of alienation is even more prominent than in drama. W.B. Yeats recorded this violent disastrous sense of historical alienation and presented a world where "things fall apart" and the "centre cannot hold"[3] Such a statement has definite metaphysical overtones, implying the disintegration of values in the modern world. Recognition of man's basic loneliness in an open-ended universe is seen. Modern life revealed a spiritual impotence and a tragic breakdown of human communication and this began to occupy the focal point of attention in a number of literary works.

One of the major areas in which almost all the dramatists in general and the absurdists in particular, engage themselves in the theme of alienation is estrangement. The guilt of sin, breakdown in family and friendly relationships or any other detrimental problems of the human psyche are responsible for estrangement in the modern world. It is always associated with the loneliness of man and his self. Man, particularly modern man, is totally estranged from himself, from God, his fellow men and nature. O'Neill has been identified as the pioneer who indicated the theme of alienation through *The Hairy Ape.* Yank, the hero of the play, is a modern Everyman who denies the moral security of his life as a stocker and sets out to rediscover where he belongs to, in his struggle, against an unfriendly, indifferent, blind and amoral universe. Tennessee Williams has handled this theme in *The Glass Menagerie* through the portrayal of a family where every one of them is shown as looking pathologically inward when they become conscious of their solitude resulting out of their lack of nerve and love among them. Arthur Miller has delineated this same theme in his *The Death of Salesman,* through Willy Loman to whom the society dictated alienation, who in turn alienated himself by his blind submission to material aspirations and false illusions. Albee successfully continues the significant American dramatic tradition of O'Neill, Miller and Williams.

The above illustrations indicate that alienation arises out of two factors:

(i) either by segregation of one's own self owing to one's failure to love his neighbor (Biblical sense) or to establish a genuine communication and contact with the neighbor; or

(ii) by the segregation imposed on oneself owing to various factors namely class, race, religion, politics etc.

Albee's plays are not simple because they function at different levels. The characters almost infect us with their moods while revealing their own complex worlds, where schizophrenia, loneliness and dying are based on sense of alienation. From The Zoo Story, alienation became a powerful theme of Albee's dramatic statement on 'human condition'. The human condition in America from 60's as Albee sees it, is a capitulation to the fear of not being loved and the attendant failure to love. The result is a strong sense of emptiness, loss and the tendency to alienate oneself not only from the fellow human beings, but also from what otherwise would have been an innervated and self confident belief in one's own self and through natural warmth and love.

Albee's first play, The Zoo Story, one of the most significant American plays, presents a circular pattern of fear and alienation each leading to the other in a vicious circle. However, in the narrative content and the structural pattern of dramatic elements, The Zoo Story goes back to the naturalistic cry of O'Neill's *The Hairy Ape* against the social alienation and divisiveness generated by the American capitalist system.

The Zoo Story is fundamentally a drama of social criticism, a parable of the two different alienated souls, a social spectrum coloring the consequences of apathy and human indifference, and revealing the self-destructiveness and the cruelty present in the society. Jerry, the protagonist in The Zoo Story, is alienated by society and himself not only because of some inner weakness but also because of the evils of the social milieu. Jerry is a victim of circumstances and the norms of bourgeois society. As the only child of his parents, discarded by them when he was very young (the mother walked out on the father and "good old pop" took to drinking and died a few months later), brought up by an aunt for some years who also "dropped dead on the stairs to her apartment ... on the afternoon of his high school education"[4] (P. 177), Jerry has lived a lonely life almost since his birth. With his home in one of the "sickening rooming houses on the west side of New York City "which is the greatest city in the world." (P. 177) The irony is that the "the greatest city in the world" has apartments like the one Jerry is living in, which is a picture of dissolution and vacuity. The occupants of the house, live their own separate lives like the way "animals exist with each other and with people too ... everyone separated by bars from everyone else". (P. 179) Fellow feeling, brotherhood, love, personal relationships all have been replaced by disinterestedness and indifference and Jerry, although is aware of the problems, can do nothing about it.

Jerry, representative of the alienated-the 'permanent transient', 'the outsider' is presented as a man incapable of love.[5] Gililbert Debaucer observes: "He is the eternal vagabond, a one-night lover, the inhabitant of a top-floor of a house in a rundown neighborhood between Columbus Avenue and Central Park".[6] Jerry desires to love and to be the object of love but in vain. He has become incapable of love, of giving himself in the normal sense, with understanding: "... Where? It would be A START? Where better to make a beginning ... to understand and just possibly be understood ... a beginning of an understanding". (P. 43)

Jerry has an "infinite capacity for love" and yet it is surprising that he always fails to achieve communication ... with the dog, with the pretty little ladies" (P. 167) whom he can love only once and with Peter. To remove isolation it is necessary not only to love but also to be loved. The whole episode featuring the Landlady's dog and his own encounter with it leaves Jerry a man of insight and experience but he desperately wants to communicate with someone that he decides to try the same method with Peter. He first tries words to make Peter remain with him by bribing him with assurance by telling him stories of the dog and the zoo. The entire drama stages Jerry in fear of being alone again.

In Edward Albee's world inadequacy of language, leads to lack of communication. Communication is evaded in order to avoid confrontation with the truth. Therefore Peter feigns indifference to whatever Jerry tells him as he is afraid of facing the truth of existence. He is totally engulfed in his mask of illusions of a happy, contended life and prefers to remain aloof. Jerry fails to realize that his use of words add to his isolation rather than alleviate it. On one occasion Peter complains to Jerry, "you don't really carry on a conversation; you just ask questions" (P. 163). Jerry is similar to Albee's other protagonists in his reliance on words, "unable to 'relate' ... (they) look to language to forge whatever identity and relationships their lives have lacked".[7] Language does not help communication between Peter and Jerry, Jerry tries physical contact. The last strategy that Jerry employs is to make Peter defend his bench. The story of Jerry and the dog is repeated with a reversal of roles for Jerry, for he is now the dog and Peter is Jerry. The method of physical contact begins, and Jerry makes Peter fight for his territory, his exclusive possession which is very valuable for him. He has come here for 'years' and has had "hours of great pleasure, great satisfaction", (P. 182) right here. The usually calm Peter is aroused ultimately to defend his bench. He fights with the same ferocity that the dog had shown, he becomes almost beastlike, a savage fighting for a bone. To evenly match Jerry tosses over a knife at Peter's feet and feels that in the role of a murderer Peter may have a sense of oneness with him. When he himself falls on the knife held in Peter's hand he succeeds in establishing contact. This has not been easy for; "to establish contact one must reach below the surface to the level of pain and pleasure, to the animal core".[8] Jerry has succeeded in 'teaching 'Peter with 'kindnesses' and 'cruelty'.

Jerry's isolation is removed finally as well as Peter's. It is not only Jerry who is alienated from society: Peter, too represents the modern alienated man, although his isolation is self-imposed of which he is unaware. Peter is separated from his own animal nature: the bars that separate him from his own nature and from other people are his material possessions and his traditions. He himself is responsible for his isolation. He has everything that a man would wish to be successful and happy in life, yet he shields himself with a barrier that is not easy to break.

The title of the play suggest two things: on the surface level it is just a story that Jerry narrates of what happened at the Zoo, and on the other it is the symbolic level where the society can be looked at as a Zoo in which human beings, like animals, are separated from one another by bars. Man is living in a cage in which communication is not possible. Isolation, loneliness and frustration are, in fact, major subjects in this realistic and symbolical drama of "a lonely outcast who tries to make contact with another human being and who finally binds himself to that in death".[9] In his loneliness and frustration Jerry is not hesitant to even risk his life for some sort of communication. Edward Albee suggests here:

> ... the essence of the life of Jerry and his kind is solitude, separation and captivity inside one's own skin ... physical contact is only a palliative and not a lasting remedy for the solitude to which we are all condemned.[10]

Solitude can be removed only by love and this emotion has long been erased from the hearts of human beings. Selfishness, hatred, insincerity and apathy have taken its place in the modern mechanistic age. Man and his feelings have been reduced to a machine. Existing in such a society automatically brings in alienation.

In The Death of Bessie Smith, Albee presents a different theme of alienation. It is racial alienation. By creating convincing dramatic situations, Albee communicates through this play the horrors of a civilization that has lost its human content and reality in preference to a make-believe structure. The emotional insufficiency of the individual and the pressures of the society that distorts the real response to life are substantiated through a social injustice, namely racism.

Edward Albee has accurately presented before his audience a picture of the death of Bessie Smith as a result of the cruelty, callousness and inhumanity of the Whites who reject the plea of her Black friend to provide emergency treatment to her as she lay bleeding to death in her car. The contrast between the lives of the Blacks and the Whites is or hang-ups about anything as Whites have. They are simple human beings without any malice even though they are evident from the various events of the play. The Blacks have no sense of isolation, no frustration as the oppressed class.

Albee generates his ideas from the all-pervasive factor of isolation among people, arising out of inhumanity. The barriers of class, race, religion and politics put people into cages which close them off from the possibility of growth which will enable them to live fully and really. Albee substantiates that men and women are the accomplices in the creation of their own unhappiness and dissatisfactions because they fail to fill up the places emptied by necessity and time with understanding and acceptance, as well as with openness for new experiences and continuous unselfish concern for people around them in different stages of their lives. Unable to attain the apparent consolations in the private life, the individual turns only to the arbitrary systems of the public world -the assertion of social patterns of scientific principles invoked to deny chaos. But such a coding of order decays human richness, dignity and grandeur based on good relationships, and communal harmony. Albee's finding is that alienation becomes an all-pervasive canker in such a rosy life.

Mainly the play The Death of Bessie Smith is about the collapse of human values and national purpose. In other words as Stenz observes, it is an

> ... exploration of the effects which the rigid institution have on the development of the individual ... he is particularly concerned with the consequences for everyone involved in a climate of living which fosters racisms.[11]

The Nurse in the play is a typical example of a neurotic woman frustrated with her life, away from the outer world in general, and in search of her being .She lives in a small enclosed world of the hospital where she works at the admission desk caught up in a mesh of false values and racism, she lives in a fictitious realm trapped in her own myths. She had done nothing constructive to help herself to make life bearable either for herself or for others. She articulates her utter despair: "... but that is the way things are."[12] (P. 88) She never attempts to foster ideas of her own or take a stand, but seeks refuge in the established, simplistic fictions. Thus frustrated and left alone she is devoid of the language of tenderness and trust, neither at home nor at the hospital. As Stenz observes, "She is only capable of the most primitive kind of human interaction, one that is based on a power struggle and leaves no room for love-love that is not doled out as a compensation or used as a weapon"[13]

The Nurse takes pleasure in parading her superior position as a White before the Black Orderly and tries to give vent to her frustrations by laughing at him. She amuses herself by humiliating the Orderly, assigning him degrading errands, reminding him that the needs of the Negro patients comes second in the hospital's priority. In her desperation to rid herself of the monotonous shape that her life has taken she contemplates marrying even a Negro. She is in a confused state of mind as she is unable to decide what she wants from life or from other people. The Nurse is trapped in a cage; "White sepulcher in which (she) is writhing"[14] and does not have any visible means of escape. For her, there is no ideal solution to dream about, no place where things will be better; no escape. She advises Orderly to go up North, to New York City, "where nobody's any better than anybody else", (P. 95) but that will be no solution for his or her problem of alienation.

Reality works on a different plane for the Nurse. She is wrapped up in illusions and would like things to be different from what they are. When she can take it no longer, she lefts out an agonized cry:

> ... I am sick ... I am sick of everything in his hot, stupid fly-ridden world, I am sick of the disparity between things as they are, and as they should be! I am sick of this desk ... This uniform ... it scratches ... I am sick of the sight of you ... the though of you makes me itch ... I am sick of him. I am sick of talking to people on phone in his damn hospital ... I am sick of the smell of Lysol ... I could die of it ... I am sick of going to bed and I am sick of waking up ... I am tired ... I am tired of the truth ... and I am tired of lying about the truth ... I am tired of my skin ... I WANT OUT." (p. 124)

This is unfortunately a cry in vain for her. She has no way out and no one is to be blamed for this than she herself. In the words of Luke Grande,

> ... she could be any contemporary neurotic surrounded by Twentieth century alienation and jobbing the world around her into recognition of her existence.[15]

and not succeeding much. The entire problem of the Nurse and the cause of her frustration is that she has an intense desire to be recognized in society. This does not appear to be possible for her as she was unable to make create a world for herself.

When Bessie Smith is brought into the White hospital for help, the Nurse is unable to free herself of her prejudices and conventional hatred towards the Blacks by which she is completely bound and anxious that the Intern too acts in the same manner by refusing to do anything for the Negro Bessie. But the Intern is not as inhuman as she is and despite all protestations from her, he goes out to see whether he can serve the injured Negro woman. He comes back shocked finding that she had already died before arriving at the hospital. The Nurse turns hysterical with her laughter mounting up to hysteria, she mocks the Intern, "Great ... White Doctor ... You are finished. You have had your last patient here ... a nigger ... a dead nigger lady ... WHO SINGS". (P. 136) The incident is nerve shattering for all the three characters present .The Nurse had an alternative, a very good opportunity to break those shackles binding her, but she lacked inner strength and so suffers. Her alienation is complete.

The duality of the Nurse is simply amazing. She has no qualms about listening to and enjoying Bessie Smith sing, but when she is required for help, she steps back proud of her superior position and also has the nerve to say, "Oh! This is no plain woman ... this is no ordinary nigger ... this is Bessie Smith!" (P. 135) Accepting the values around her while at the same time despising them, she lives in a state of dangling disharmony with her existence. She is left alone to continue death-in-life situation.

The Nurse makes the Orderly also another victim of her ridicule. His alienation is greater than the nurses' as his is living and working amongst the Whites, away from his 'brethren'. He tries to please everybody, but succeeds in isolating himself from all. His legitimate desire to find his place under the sun is transformed into a submissive opportunism. But things were not as easy as he imagines. He himself is the cause of his alienation, since he has taken up this job as the first step on the ladder of success, knowing fully well the status of Blacks in a White community. The glamour of the world of the Whites has so enamored the Orderly that he has lost all sense of brotherhood for his own people. He is typical example of an opportunist who can go length for self-advancement alienating from his own people.

Who's Afraid of Virginia Woolf? one of the most powerful of Edward Albee's plays has almost all his major themes incorporated into it. Albee has provided a genuine study on alienation in two couples: George and Martha, and Nick and Honey. Alienation, as it is seen in this play, is of people who are firmly attached to one another as they are, hostile to one another and whose hostility rises out of the conditions of their attachment. The insults and the abuses that George and Martha hurl at each other are not the result of their having found peace and love somewhere else, not because there is no love involved in their marriage, but because they themselves have not grown as people. They have remained static in their lives, have not developed their personalities and have done nothing to merit success in society. Out of the awareness of this flaw in themselves, they attack each other savagely, blaming each other for the cause. Both are aware of the shortcoming of each other and none lets the other forget them.

George has surrendered his intellectual integrity by refusing to play college politics. He no longer has the capacity to make an honest intellectual contribution. He has not utterly demeaned himself but what should have remained a passionate interest in life has dwindled him to do just a "job". He is alienated from himself and from his gifts just as factory worker is alienated from his own labor, which gives him no satisfaction but looms over him like a hostile force.

It is not only George who has failed, but Martha also reviles him for his failures. Martha's 'sado-masochism' and her feelings of hostility are because of her desire for domination and frustration. Frustration awakens the feelings of hostility and the hostile feelings themselves arouse anxiety. Her problems arise from the development of an idealized self-image. She has learnt to conceive of herself as the 'earth-mother'-the symbol of fertility and sexuality that the decedent New Carthage society encourages. She has also built for herself the image of the "man in the house", the dominant woman. In all these processes, Martha becomes estranged from her real self ... which is quiet simple, unassuming and submissive. As Stenz observes:

> Her intelligence and imagination undirected, her great energy dissipated in vain, vicarious living, Martha is not only of her lack of self-esteem but also of her own thwarted aggressiveness".[16]

Continuous frustration in private and public life has been leading her to seek refuge in heavy drinking, promiscuity-a series of crummy, totally pointless infidelities. Instead of making her life meaningful from what is left she is still 'walking what's left of her wits'. Missing no opportunity to make an eye-catching spectacle of herself, she reminds the young man on campus that, if she is not the wife of the man who runs the History Department she is the daughter of the college President and therefore a 'somebody' to be reckoned with. As she grows older and older her sluggishness also grows. She is driven to hold on to her illusions more tightly. It is her pains that make her ruthlessly egotistical. Her emotional instability and aggressive attitude do not allow her to spare George whose professional failure crushed her major dreams. Especially she cannot tolerate his passive indifference. He shows indifference even when Martha flirts Nick in their own house with his knowledge.

Thus their mutual disregard takes them out of genuine relationship with each other. Their insensible egoism and lack of communication has made them combatants than life-partners. Alienation thus becomes less an aspect of their human situation than their inauthentic response to that situation. Bigsby points out that "... far from facilitating human contact, illusions rather alienate individuals from one another and serve to emphasize their separation".[17] Gilbert Debauccer observes:

> Albee does not say that external reality is sufficient to justify his characters retreat; it is also weakness and their inability to create for themselves a unity, a career, a child; their cowardice; and compromises that have reduced them to this plight"[18]

Nick and Honey are also alienated from each other due to lack of communication between them. Though they have known each other since childhood, yet their marriage rests not on love or faith but on deceit. From the beginning George spots Nick for an opportunist who married Honey because he thought she was pregnant and because she had money. He agrees to make love to Martha, the fifty-two year old woman, perhaps with the hope that satisfying Martha would help him to sustain a close personal rapport with the President, her father. Being highly materialistic and totalitarian in his values, he is interested in power. Hoping to establish a dystopia, he has constituted his own illusory world detaching himself from what he is and where he is, as George does by reading his books. However either way they have suffered from "gradual ... going to sleep of the brain cells ..." (P. 93)

Honey's problem in life is her fear of bearing children and she prevents herself having them by using some measures unknown to Nick. Their lives are alienated from part of themselves, have become empty and meaningless. Nick and Honey have a problem relating to each other which has affected their married life. Through this play Albee presents an inter-family alienation and links it to a genuine, significant social situation ... that of the success myth.

Anxiety and alienation transcend the purely human realm and assume a metaphysical dimension in Tiny Alice and the sexual undercurrents of this alienation and frustration become far more a potent force. Having accepted faith out of the fear of loneliness and helplessness in his childhood, Julian expects a continual reassurance from the faith and religion that embodies the faith, against the growing threats to his dependence from a variety of human urges - egoistic, emotive and even sexual. The delicately maintained sanity through this dependence stands threatened when his religious faith fails to subsume his growing human urges.

Brother Julian in Tiny Alice lives an isolated life because of his failure to adapt himself to the truth of life. Julian's creation of an imaginary son of God, as creator and mover, does not coincide with the popular view of God as a kind of miracle worker. He committed himself to an asylum because his faith in God left him, which in turn was brought on by the manner in which people mock God. He has a "confused and intimidated"[20] (P. 60) contact with it. The years in the asylum marked the heightening alienation from himself for he had been living in his dependence on his religious faith. During his stay at the asylum, he remained completely isolated from the outside world. He describes the way he felt during the period.

> I ... declined. I ... shriveled into myself; a glass dome ... descended, and it seemed I was out of reach, unreachable, finally unreaching, in this ... paralysis, of sorts. (P. 43)

His life was at a standstill all those six years when his faith abandoned him. Unable to open his heart to reach anyone, he gradually recoiled more and more into himself and became unreachable to others too. He built a wall around him that could not be broken into. At moments he would be gripped with hallucinations, fantasies and day-dreams, some of which were sexual in nature. He confides in Miss Alice he could not sort out his "imaginings from what was real," (P. 61) like the incident when he thought he had been intimate with a woman he met at the mental home.

After six years in the asylum, Julian was persuaded eventually to believe that he was over concerned by hallucinations, some of which was inevitable and also desirable. He was, therefore, discharged from there. Julian was back into the world in the same state as he was when he went to the mental home. His hallucinations were still troubling him and his faith in God has not returned. The religious faith that he started as a simple answer to his loneliness and helplessness becomes in the course of time an egoistical craving for martyrdom and sacrifice.

Julian is guilty of living a corpse-like life. His career is nothing but a series of evasions; his refusal to pronounce final vows and his desire to remain in the service of the church; his rejection of God as he is presented by men and his creation of a more personal God; his desire to serve and his doubt about the usefulness of his sacrifice; all these are evidences of Julian's alienation from his society. He is a man whose God is slain and not replaced. He is unable to make a real commitment and avoids conflict and confrontation when they arise.

In Miss Alice's castle, Julian is given several opportunities to question the situation he is in, but he remains willfully blind to the trap that is being set for him. His first reaction is to escape once again to the asylum, "my refuge ... in the world, from all the demons waking, my REFUGE!" (P. 170) He feels he was better off there. He could at least work according to his desires and not be dictated to by anyone else. He resists acceptance and refuses to stay behind with the model of the castle and let others depart. Julian becomes a martyr then, with the Lawyer taking the last step ... of shooting him. He is sacrificed to Alice! God and the grant to the church are accomplished. The innocent is destroyed by the corrupt. Everyone goes away leaving Julian stranded to ponder on his responses to life. He ultimately (but too late) realizes that there is nothing that can protect man from his lonely condition. Neither faith nor relationships are adequate to remove his loneliness. He has to look within himself for the causes for his isolated state and remove them. Had Julian been more aware of what was going on around him, had he been well versed and clever in the affairs of the world, he would not have met this fate. He himself is responsible for his alienation. He tried to be different from others by holding a separate idea of God and refused to accept the God created by man. As a result he suffers and finally is made to accept what he had insisted he wanted ... union with the abstraction.

Unlike Peter, Jerry, Tobias and others, Julian's isolation is not removed and he dies an alienated man. Although he does try to involve himself in the affairs of others and mix with the outside world, that does not help him in any way. He remains an isolated man till the very last breath of his life.

In A Delicate Balance, Tobias alienation is like Peter's-self-imposed, caused by his own nature. In his own home and in the social order to which he should belong, he is an alien, suffering from a gnawing sense of disorientation. Normally a self-conscious person, Tobias after his retirement, settles comfortably in the suburbs with his wife and sister-in-law. Never was he interested in showing interest in home affairs and he whiles away his time in such past time as playing golf and listening to Bruneker as Peter amuses himself by reading books, away from home. On the whole Tobias life appears to be running smoothly. He has been an excellent provider and a "good husband"[21] (P. 6) as Agnes describes him. Everything would have gone on as usual in this family had not two unexpected things taken place simultaneously one evening - the return of their prodigal daughter after the failure of her fourth marriage and the arrival of friends to seek refuge in their home. These two parallel events bring out the true nature of Tobias and his relationship with his family members as well as his friends.

Tobias-a man of few words himself, his character is mostly revealed through the dialogues of other people. Claire calls him 'predictable, incapable of passion, stolid, Tobias'. (P. 16) and he is satisfied to be that, for this means security for him as it lacks any kind of commitment. He withdraws from what he sees especially the harsher realities of life. He gives up that to love is to become vulnerable. He is unable to adjust to the pain of the death of his son, Teddy at the age of two and chooses rather to substitute a kind of painless existence. Such a reaction leads directly to that retreat into himself, which Albee identifies as 'the demise of intensity, the private preoccupations, the substitutions" (P. 82) Tobias fails to give his daughter the reassurance that she was still loved after the birth of her brother. Agnes recalls how 'she felt unwanted, tricked, (P. 110) Perhaps the son meant a lot to Tobias. After the death of Teddy, Tobias retires to seclusion of his own room severing all physical relations from his wife for fear of going through the pain of loss once again. He has never been able to establish rapport with Julia.

Tobias' cat, which had lived with him contentedly for fifteen years, had all of a sudden withdrawn its affection refusing to stay in the same room with him, refusing even to purr. Tobias describes how he had become progressively determined to restore their relationship. His failure in his attempts at the restoration of their love turned his affection into hatred. He felt betrayed. Love had turned into a kind of hate, a need to destroy the cat rather than face something in him, which could account for its behavior. He got the cat killed so that it could not reproach him. But now he realizes that it is precisely his failure to persevere in love merely because it is not returned which is the source of his sense of guilt. Wrapped up in his own self concern, he had been unable to recognize the urgent need for love and compassion in a world unspeakably bleak without them. Now, in retrospect, he concludes, "I might have tried harder. I might have gone on, as long as cats live" (P. 37) This is essentially the obligation in which he has equally failed with Julia, Agnes and will fail in his response to his best friends who force him to the point of involvement. In the course of the play he gradually feels his way towards an understanding, both of the fact of his own isolation and of the real nature of his relationship with those he had taken to be his best friends. He finally admits that he does not love them and confesses they are a threat to his peace of mind. He applies the lesson of his own parable to himself, by a supreme effort of will.

Agnes's life, too, is a gaping tomb. Once a "splendid cocoon," (P. 68) as she describes herself, she responds to love, and was full of feminine sensitivity; she appears before us in the action of the play as a "drill sergeant, a "perfectionist", a "harridan", the "ruler of roost." Her transformation, however, is not entirely the doing of her husband. As Gilbert Porter remarks:

> He sowed the seeds, it is true, but they fell on fertile ground ... linked together in their flawed humanity, the two exist in a love-hate relationship typical of Albee's characters.[22]

The 'rolling pleasant land', is deeply scarred. In the face of an imbecile husband, a dead son, a hysterical daughter, and a drunken sister, Agnes tends to lose her own balance. In her first speech she describes her hypothetical insanity as "sending the balloon adrift", (P. 7) obviously she wants to remain placidly uninvolved in the world. However she cannot remain non-committal like Tobias: she becomes a bitter spectator, something of a chorus and a shrew, rolled into one. Ultimately, she resigns herself to her inevitable emptiness:

> Time happens, I suppose ... To people. Everything becomes ... too late, finally. You know it's going on ... up on the hill; and you can see the dust, and hear the cries, and the steel ... but you wait; and time happens. When you do go, sword, shield ... finally ... there's nothing there ... save rust; bones; and the winds. (P. 90)

As escapism serves no purpose other than intensifying the agony of alienation in human relationship, Agnes tries to submerge the agony of alienation from people under the dull, monotony of routine life facing the facts of life as a matter of habit. Agnes chooses neither to fight her marital alienation by trying to win Tobias affection nor allows herself to be frustrated into seeking an escape into loneliness.

Agnes has willfully withdraws herself in taking the decision in the matter of Harry and Edna's stay and forces Tobias to decide for himself. Not having ever taken an independent decision in family matters, Tobias is very perturbed at the idea. In a moment of frustration he accuses Agnes of "copping out!" (P. 132) which she admits of doing but only because her motto has been to 'follow', she lets her man "decide the moral issues" (P. 132) Tobias doesn't have much choice before him but to decide one way or other, either to let Harry and Edna stay back or to get rid of the "whole bunch" (P. 141) of Agnes, Julia and Claire. So he does something 'rare' for the family, he thinks; he fights to overcome his own self interest and in doing so goes some way towards expiating his sense of guilt. He tells Harry: "I DON'T WANT YOU HERE! I DON'T LOVE YOU! BUT BY GOD ... YOU STAY!!" (P. 162) In accepting the reality Tobias has, in a way atoned for his guilt and his isolation, is somewhat removed in the end .After the departure of Harry and Edna when he apologies to his family and comes close to both his wife and his daughter. Their relationship comes to calling each other 'Pop' and 'Julie'. Tobias who would prefer to be in his shell, not willing to communicate with anyone, would hopefully now come out of his imposed isolated state and mix with everybody as a normal human being. Even his friends will not be a 'strangers' to him any longer.

Tobias' alienation is caused by guilty complex within him, of not being able to fulfill his role as a husband and father properly. He tries to avoid contact with others as he feels he would turn out to be a failure in their eyes once they come very close to him. He does not try to love because of the commitment involved in love, which in his view leads only to pain and isolation. This is evident in his relationship with his cat. Agnes makes a very profound observation on the killing of the cat. She says, "There was nothing to be done; there was no ... meeting between you" (P. 26) Putting her to death was the most natural thing to do because of the lack of communication between Tobias and her. Fortunately, in Tobias' relationship with others, the situation does not reach this extreme stage and before anything disastrous happens, Tobias realizes his mistake.

Edward Albee has dealt with one of the most crucial aspects of modern man's condition by presenting his alienation and the cause of this alienation. Albee is deeply sensitive about the situation of modern man and would like some changes to be brought within them. Like other writers before him and like his contemporaries, Albee accurately is aware of this problem in modern society. As has been said before, alienation is neither new nor an unexplored subject in the literary area. Every writer has dealt with it according to his own perception and understanding of it. Albee mainly puts forth socially and self-alienated individuals in themselves or of social ills.

Examples of self-alienated characters are found in the form of Peter, Nurse, George, Martha Tobias and Julian and Himself. These characters are isolated from their families and their surroundings mainly because they live in a world of illusions refusing to face the harsh facts of life. Their basic tendency is escapism and evasion. They lack moral courage. Instead of allowing any kind of change to affect their lives, they are contented to live in the world they have created for themselves. As a result these characters find it difficult to relate to the other. Contact with others appears to be impossible for them. Words are inadequate to serve their purpose. Albee feels that there is hope for them because contact is not impossible but is being evaded to avoid confrontation of truth. If they try hard they can communicate. The characters in Albee's plays are not allowed to remain passive and apathetic; they have to find out a way on their own to bring about satisfaction and happiness in their lives. Some of the characters like George and Martha and Tobias are able to destroy their illusions and complexes and as such face the truth bravely. Very few characters in Albee's plays remain isolated till the end, the reason being that Albee urges his characters to break away from fantasies and confront life as it is. This confrontation leads them to become normal human beings with a capacity to exist harmoniously with others in society. In rare cases, if the characters do not remove their alienation, e.g. the Nurse and Julian or the family in The American Dream, it is because their hold on their ideals and false values is so strong that they fail to realize the absurdity of their situation. Such people are beyond cure. Mommy and Daddy have been leading meaningless existence all their lives and this has become reality for them. They cannot visualize any state other than this and hence make no efforts to change.

The contemporary society, with men estranged from one another, with the collapse of values, has become a symbol of alienation. Confrontation with the real human situation pressurizes the alienated individuals to experience the anguish of loneliness:

> Man is torn away from the primary union with nature, which characterizes animal existence. Having at the same time reason and imagination, he is aware of his loneliness and separateness ...[23]

They are like Hamlet in Shakespeare's drama that withdraw themselves and move around in a world of their own, musing over their selves. The barriers of isolation are not to be broken; the individuals are not prepared to suffer the pangs of pain that may be cause by the shattering of illusions.

The themes of alienation and non-communication have been the pre-occupation of Albee and the anguish caused by alienation is distinct in his plays. Albee believes that the human beings who are gregarious in nature are in fact lonely entities. They have focused attention on the suffering 'loners' and their desperate attempts to hold on to something. They appear to share Sartre's belief of human existence in a changing world, that there is "No more characters, heroes are freedoms caught in a trap like all of us."[24] Individuals in the modern world are ensnared by the institutions of the society.

Albee is not in the habit of suggesting antidotes to alienation for he believes that a temporary remedy is not at all the solution to this malady. To achieve a lasting relief one has to be courageous and patient. In this he is very unlike Strindberg and Ionesco who consider man's alienated condition to be a permanent feature of human life. They nowhere suggest that an end can be but to this sorry state of affairs. A similarity between Ionesco and Albee can be found in their views that words are ineffective for the purposes of communication. People cannot be other than strangers for most of the time they do nothing but utter clichés from which all sense has evaporated.

Like Tennessee Williams, Albee expresses his indignation against an insensitive society by projecting alienated characters. Most of his characters are alienated because of external circumstances and being a social critic, Albee does not let go this opportunity to expose social evils that are responsible for man's condition. In Bessie Smith case, it is the most hideous over all evils ... apartheid; in Jerry's it is the vast gap between the upper and lower classes of society and also the general apathy in modern man. For Edward Albee, Alienation is a serious problem, but not one that is without remedy.

REFERENCES

1. Samuel Coledridge *The Rime of Ancient Mariner*, qtd. Dr. Raghukul Tilak, Rama Publications, 1977.

2. Murray Levin, *Political Alienation*, Man Alone Eric and Mary Josephson, ed., (New York: Dell Publishing Co., Inc., 1962), p. 227.

3. W.B.Yeats, *The Second Coming*, Selected Poems, (London, 1956), p. 15.

4. Edward Albee: *The Zoo Story, The Death of Bessie Smith, The Sandbox*, Three Plays introduced by the Author. (New York: Coward, Mc Cann and Geoghegan Inc. New York 1959).

5. M.Nilan Mary, *Albee's The Zoo Story: Alienated man and Nature of Love*, Modern Drama XVI, June 1973, No. 1, p. 56.

6. Gilbert Debaussccer, *Edward Albee: Tradition and Renewal*, Trans, D.Anee Williams (Brussels: American Studies Center, 1967), p. 10.

7. Arthur Oberg, *Edward Albee: His Language and Imagination*, Prairie Schooner, (Spring, 1066), p. 143.

8. Rose A. Zimbardo, *Symbolism and Naturalism in Edward Albee's: The Zoo Story*, A Collection of Critical Essays ed., C.W.E. Bigsby, p. 48.

9. Ruby Cohn and Benard F Dukore, *Twentieth Century of the Contemporary Theatre*, rev. ed. (New York: Random House, 1966), p. 650.

10. Gilbert Debusscer, *Edward albee: Tradition and Renewal*, Trans. A.D.Williams (Brussels. American Studies Centre, 1967) p. 14.

11. Anita Maria Stenz, *Edward Albee: The Poet of Loss*, (The Hague: Mouton, 1978) p. 14.

12. Edward Albee: *The Zoo Story, The Death of Bessie Smith, The Sandbox*, Three Plays Introduced by the Author. (New York: Coward, Mc Cann and Geoghegan Inc. New York 1959).

13. Anita Maria Stenz, *Edward Albee: The Poet of Loss*, (The Hague: Mouton, 1978) pp. 16-17.

14. James Baldwind, *Theatre: The Negro In and Out of it,* Beyond the Angry Black, John A Williams, ed., (New York: Cooper Square Publishers, 1966), p. 9.

15. Edward Albee's Bessie Smith, *Alienation 'The Color Problem*, Drama Critique, Volume V, No. 2 (May, 1962), p. 66.

16. Anita Maria Stenz, *Edward Albee: The Poet of Loss*, (The Hague: Mouton, 1978) p. 42.

17. C.W.E. Bigsby, *Confrontation and Commitment: A Study of Contemporary American Drama* (London, 1967) p. 47.

18. Gilbert Debaussccer, *Edward Albee: Tradition and Renewal*, Trans. A.D.Williams (Brussels. American Studies Centre, 1967) p. 50.

19. Edward Albee, *Who is Afraid of Virginia Woolf?* (Great Britain: Penguin Books, 1983).

20. Edward Albee, *Tiny Alice*, Atheneum, (New York, 1965).
21. Edward Albee, *A Delicate Balance*, Atheneum, (New York, 1967).
22. *Tobys Last Stand: The Evanescence of Commitment in A Delicate Balance*, Educational Theatre Journal, 31.3 (October 1979) 400.
23. Eric Fromn, *The Sane Society*, pp. 35-37, Qtd. By C.W.E. Bigsby, A Critical Introduction to Twentieth Century American Drama, II, p. 273.
24. Jean Paul Sartre quoted by L.S.Deshpande in *The Theatre of the Absurd in Marathi*, Essays on Comparative Literature and Linguistic, ed. L.S. Deshpande et. Al (New Delhi: Sterling Publishers, 1984), p. 98.

6

Techniques
The Man who had Three Arms

> It is no longer enough that a work of art be beautiful, it must be interesting. And, as a rule, in order to be interesting, it must be 'contemporary'[1]

The function of a theatre, in any age, is to reflect the times, the course of events and the behavior of the people. If logically constructed plays fail to portray the times and the people genuinely, they cease to be authentic and tend to be obtrusive. Plays, as a prism of life, through which human experiences are refracted, become images of the condition of man in a particular age and society differing in accordance with playwrights, perceptions and interpretations of the world and of the moral and social values of the time they represent.

The twentieth century has been characterized as the age of anxiety in the same sense as the seventeenth century was called the age of enlightenment; the eighteenth century the age of reason; and the nineteenth century the age of progress. The contemporary drama reflects the age of anxiety, despair and insecurity. The theatre being the most public of arts, offers the opportunity of acting out anxieties and fears which are born in the conflict between private needs and public values.

The distinctive feature of the American theatre is its relentless experimentation. Each playwright experimented in one form or another, turned from one mode or attitude to another, from the well-made plays to the loose structure or from realism to symbolism to expressionism. This experimentation was not only found in playwriting but also in acting techniques, in design, direction, lighting, and setting also.

After enjoying immense popularity till the first half of the twentieth century, American drama seemed to lag behind other genres in the first decade of the post world war II era. The death of O' Neil created vacuum in the American theatre. A breakthrough came under influence of two new European movements, the 'Theatre of Cruelty' initiated by Antonin Artaud and the 'Theatre of Absurd' by Samuel Beckett. Writers like Beckett, Brencht, Genet and the Ionesco, each unique in dramatic style laid the foundation of a new theatre. Simple and active, it created dramatic language of enormous possibility. A renewed interest in mime and gesture, silence, fantasy and simplicity contributed to fresh apprehension of reality. With Beckett's *Waiting for Godot* the reign of the do it yourself drama began. Construction was out, characterization was out, style and decency of language were out, and commitment was in.

The new dramatists were attracted towards the contradictory and mysterious quality of existence represented by the Theatre of Absurd. The bare sets, the unidentifiable characters, the meaningless jabbering, the disjointed language, the abrupt beginnings and endings of the drama of the absurd replaced the earlier conventions. The unrealistic character of these plays gave freedom to dramatists to treat non-logical situations like dreams and to communicate poetic images. The dramatist of the absurd employed, surrealism to synthesize the experience of the conscious and the unconscious minds.

With these different, colorful and powerful strands of a new movement weaving themselves together the modern dramatist no longer worked in the caged, confined dramatic traditions of the past. They were free to chose subjects and invent new dramatic forms. The result was a bewildering and staggering number of styles; poetic drama, symbolism, expressionism, the epic theatre, absurdism, surrealism, experimentalism and others. Attitudes towards stage designs and sets were similarly various. One end of the range was marked by the meticulously realistic sets of Ibsen. In every area of the cotemporary theatre, language, setting, acting, technique, theme, stage décor changed according to trends and Albee too plunged into experimentation with the same urgency and compulsive needs as other dramatists. Needless to say the result was a diverse output of talent in the field of technique. The variety which he reveals in his plays, speaks of a complex artistic mind, a mind which can be understood only through a detailed analysis of his plays.

Plot, setting and characters-all intentionally minimal, undermine the American family. Albee having directed a few of his own plays, is very particular about his settings in his plays and devises each setting strictly in accordance with requirement of subject. Setting for Albee, is not merely true to characters in a superficial sense, but actually expressive of their thoughts and emotions. Scripts of his plays are careful with blue prints for a theatrical performance, with detailed indications which is apparent in his use of stage directions which allows his theatrical vision to emerge.

Albee reduces his sets to the barest minimum in some of his plays to give them a naturalistic touch. As an absurd playwright he brings out the isolation and emptiness of relationships in his bare settings. In The Zoo Story, the stage is set with two wooden benches on either side in a lonely park. This sort of setting enhances and objectifies the feeling of isolation. The open air setting becomes functional by reflecting the mood and situation of the play. The remoteness and loneliness of the park, indicates the empty life of Peter. Moreover, the setting highlights the inhibited, reserved and vacuous nature of Peter; who invariably chooses to come to a lonely park, away from the hustle and bustle of the city, to read book in peace. The image of the Zoo pervades the play. Although frequent references are made about the Zoo by the Jerry such as, "I've been to the Zoo" (P. 159) on several occasions, yet the Zoo itself is now shown on the stage. The idea behind this image is quite evident: Jerry and Peter like animals in a Zoo are imprisoned in their own worlds separated from each other.

Albee's concentration on essentials is most clear in his little play The Sandbox where again with minimal staging, dramatizes his personal loss. The living room in The American Dream, has just enough furniture for all those present to be seated. The admission room of a hospital in The Death of Bessie Smith is furnished with very few items, a desk, a chair, a bench. Nothing superfluous is to be seen. Thus, the modern sterile world is revealed in the full glare of the arc lights. The porch in the Nurse's house is furnished with a little wicker furniture, old and worn out. This setting indicates decadence, drabness, and signs of a solely vegetative existence. Another scene of the play is set in a bare area with an invisible mirror or invisible dresses off stage. Jack addresses his remarks to an unseen Bessie Smith at the dressing table. The tangible signs of a mechanized, sterile living are highlighted here.

In The Play about the Baby - the set consists of two chairs and a rug in this room (the set), and "in there", the rest of the house: nursery, bedroom, bath etc. (offstage). In using bare sets for his plays, Albee provides striking similarities with Ionesco and Beckett. The arrangement appears to be an illustration of the increasing awareness of the dramatist towards covering the maximum effect through the barest setting.

Not always does Albee have such sets. He sometimes overloads his set, although rarely as in Tiny Alice. In Scene One, in Tiny Alice, "Ivy climbing a partial wall of huge stones", "an iron gate", "two chairs", "an elaborate bird cage with sum foliage in it and two birds, cardinals ... which need not be real (P. 3) are seen. The realistic properties in every small, yet significant detail make this scene naturalistic. There is a great deal of emphasis upon the 'huge stones, iron gate and elaborate bird cage', suggests something beyond doubt a trapped narrow world. The library of Miss Alice's has 'pillared walls', to show that she has isolated herself. She appears to be willfully imprisoned in a real life castle, shuttling herself off from vagaries of the world. Albee considers, 'floor -to ceiling, leather-bound books, a great arched doorway, a huge reading table-a phrenological head on it, a huge doll's house model of the building of which the present room is a part, (P. 23) all these are essential to give the effect of awe and majesty to Julian when he enters the castle for the first time, showing the status of an heiress as wealthy.

Albee is fond of using living rooms which recur as sets for his plays. Since most of Albee's plays deal with family like settings as The American Dream, Who's Afraid of Virginia Woolf? A Delicate Balance, The Lady from Dubuque, The Goat or Who is Syliva? and Marriage Play are all sets in living rooms. The set in the living rooms is marked by the atmosphere of depression and decline. The degenerating civilization finds voice in the setting. In this American nuclear home setting, Albee explodes his satiric bombs.

Very often, Albee resorts to a use of open sky as a backdrop. Such a setting is seen definitely in spatial terms. A Delicate Balance, opens with the back wall of the stage full of sky which varies from scene to scene; 'a hot blue, sunset, a great red-orange yellow sunset, sometimes full, sometimes but a hint' (P. 68) The various shades of the sky is an indication of the various status of the characters which are at certain times excited, optimistic or hopeful and sometimes pessimistic, depressed or disillusioned. In The Sandbox the function of the sky is to determine a fixed period of time-day time. The play opens with bright daylight and stretches to dark ... night. Through this effect Albee tries to bring out the negligence of the old generation by the new generation, the Young Man-a representative of the future.

Finding the Sun, The Sandbox, Seascape, are plays which are set on sea beach. In Seascape, sand dunes and the sea as the properties of the set are seen. Albee creates a right kind of atmosphere for the theme of evolution of man. It is from the waters of the sea that the sea-lizards emerge, reminding us of our past form, and they are now in the process of becoming human beings. The waters of the sea like the sky suggest infinity of time in which the existence of man is finite. The sea beach in The Sandbox shows naturalness although all characters are artificial with the exception of Grandma. Grandma reflects old harmony with nature, whereas the characters oppose nature and thus appear artificial. In Finding the Sun Albee situates a group of people-Americans at the beach. They are all trying to find the sun-pursuing happiness as far as they are able to.

In Quotations, deck on an ocean lines in mid-ocean is the set. The moving ship suggests the continuity to live. It is like the linking cable between the ancient past and the modern present, carrying with it all the possibilities of a future. The sea around epitomizes life. The characters on board, the ship are stationary, stagnant, and immobile. The ship represents the vivid, challenging life but the inmates contrast representing only boredom and ennui. Characters such as the long-winded lady and the minister stand out as cramped personalities against the vastness of the shop and openness of the sea.

Albee, a fastidious playwright, takes particular care to ensure that every detail of the settings of his plays is well worked. In Box, the setting is so simple, yet multiple layers of meaning unfold in the plain, straight, stark outlines in a large cube. Box, is not a new image to Albee. The invisible voice in the Box is the articulate expression of crone which comes from the nearby spectator. Its expression is the quality of life, within the life space. While it talks about the hopes in the past and the total extinction of all values in the present, it is not able to contemplate on future. The images, the voice uses in the stories it tells, are of moral depravity of everything in the modern world.

The set of Listening, is little archaic with the 'monster bear in half relief, the spigot of the fountain emerging from the mouth.' (P. 55) It implies the difference between the past and the present; between what was and what is and is related with the lives of the characters. The Man and the Woman who were once lovers, now, in the present behave like strangers. The Girl, who was earlier healthy and normal, has now turned into schizophrenic. The setting is significant in the sense that once the 'trimmed and clipped' setting for flirtation and meetings is now a forgotten, silent refuge at an institution. This fountain now becomes the site for the seminal heart searching of three beings. They reflect on their past lives and ponder over their relationships with one another. There is a dilemma of existence itself. The confusion of identities only serves to highlight the incongruity of their own selves. The inescapability of their fate underlines their static setting.

It is apparent in number of plays of Albee, that he uses light in his settings to show vivid contrast of light and shade in his plays. The alteration of light and dark is most powerfully brought out in The Sandbox. The play opens with bright daylight suggesting that Grandma is alive. Day in the conventional and metaphorical sense represents life, a life which is tangible, real, comprehensible and filled with action. The day gradually wanes to night, and when Grandma's death is fast approaching, Albee fills the stage with engulfing darkness. This darkness acts likes a shroud signifying its prosaic grimness. The characters are therefore in flux, graduating from the symbolic grimness of the dark to the brilliance of the day.

The dialect of night and day is carried still further in Who's Afraid of Virginia Woolf? The play which begins during the peak of night with vagueness, confusion, ignorance of minds of the four characters in the course of the play this darkness is removed and their minds are illuminated. Albee shows the approaching dawn which is an indication of a new beginning. The dawn brings along with it hope and dreams for better future. George and Martha, Nancy and Honey all begin a new and fresh course of their journey through life. The subdued and sober effects of the night persists in conveying the same sense of fear, annihilation, morbidity and depression in A Delicate Balance, The Lady from Dubuque and in Who's Afraid of Virginia Woolf?

Albee also utilizes the different positions of the sun and the sky for symbolic purposes. The sunset usually carries with it the traditional meaning of death. The rise of the sun represents rebirth or the beginning of a new life. In The Death of Bessie Smith the blazing sunset at the end of the play symbolizes the spiritual death of the Intern, Nurse and the Orderly.

Albee makes use of light in his settings not merely as structural device but also as a means to suggest an inner state of mind. The 'ebbing fire' in the fire place in All Over suggests the extinguishing light of the dying man's life. The brightest steady flame suggests the dominance of life whereas the 'ebbing fire' in dying embers corresponds with the idea of a fast declining life. Julian's predicament in Tiny Alice when he is left alone after his wedding is likened by the Butler to a little boy on whom the closed door shuts "locking him, in the dark." (P. 32) The fear in his mind is suggested by the reference of the dark closed room. Darkness suggests here a shady obscurity, a malignant fate as well as the traditional meaning of death.

Light stands for dispelling of gloom, for radiance and brightness. This effect is brought out in number of plays. The dawn in Who's Afraid of Virginia Woolf? and A Delicate Balance suggests the beginning of life. The artificial lights in the departmental store in The American Dream substitute the man-made artificial light for the natural light of god. The people of modern age appear as deceptive as the colors do under arc lamps. They are pretentious, hypocritical, and false and lack the warmth and brightness of the natural light. Albee makes use of artificial light in his setting to reveal the inevitable tendency of the modern man to be entrapped in the false show of glitter.

Quite often Albee considers his settings as an area of visualized performance. His attempts are to give a clear idea of what his mind sees as a set:

> The set for this play will vary naturally, as stage vary,... from theatre to theatre. The suggestions are just as guide, a general idea as the what author "sees" (The Death of Bessie Smith)

> I see a fairly short wall, and two sides wall angling from it to the proscenium. (Counting the Ways)

Albee's sets are therefore integral to the themes of his plays. The full value of Albee's plays does not emerge until it is seen in its relation to the settings. It is through the setting that Albee visualizes, implies, suggests or creates the very sense of the play. Albee always suggests through setting a complete psychological corresponding of the experiences of life.

Involvement of music has influenced the writings of Albee in the Theatre. Albee himself says, "I've been involved in one way or another with serious music ever since childhood. And I do think, or rather I sense that there is a relationship-at least in my own work-between dramatic structure, the form and sound and shape of a play, and the equivalent structure in music ... I find that when my plays are going on well, they seem to resemble pieces of music."[2]

In the play The Sandbox the arrangement of the stage suggests a performance where Mommy and Daddy occupy two chairs facing the audience, while a third faces in from stage towards the left side of the music stand for the musician. In the fourth scene which is enacted at the depth of night, the musician plays through nearly the entire scene but music is kept nice and soft at the suggestion of Grandma. The fourth rumble is characterized in Albee's stage direction as 'violent'- the sound of the fog-horn implies the closure to be followed by silence. Albee's use of rumbles and music is powerful here which reminds the use of music by Tennessee Williams also who calls his theatre 'Plastic Theatre' as he himself explains:

> ... extra verbal or nonliterary elements of the theatre, the various plastic elements, the purely visual things such as light and movement and color and design which play for example, such a tremendously important part in theatre ... all of these plastic things are as valid instruments of expression in the theatre as words ... [3]

Edward Albee's symbols bear symbolical overtones, a medium through which he portrays the dilemma of human existence and thus conveys his outlook on life. "Symbolism is the art of expression, ideas and emotions not by describing them directly, nor by defining them through overt comparisons with concrete images but by suggesting what these ideas and emotions are, by secreting them in mind of the reader through the use of unexplained symbols".[4]

The present man is a lonely creature left and lost in a world in which God has deserted him or in a world where there is nothing like God. Thus reason and science are illusory. The individual is trapped in a contemplation of his own image. The absurd playwrights do believe neither in the existence of God nor do they think any possibility of communication. They cannot even manage to feel that language is alive. Thus the only means left to express such a universe is through the symbols. This is the reason that the drama of the absurd tends to be extremely symbolic. It is a theater which leads to express that it is not faith but doubt that is needed to bind man with God (if there is one). Doubt and emptiness is not a drama but an exercise in acted symbols.

The deserted, unfrequented central park in The Zoo Story symbolizes the emptiness and loneliness in the life of both Peter and Jerry. To Albee the world is a zoo in which characters are forever separated by the bars of conventionality. The blazing sunset at the end of The Death of Bessie Smith is the representation of a decadent dying society - the representative of the generations. Through the symbolism Albee depicts the deaths of moral, religious and social values in society.

Albee's symbols extend across a vast range of meaning and cannot be confined to a single meaning. Certain objects, however, come to be associated with certain specific correlative and the symbolic interpretation becomes very pronounced in quiet a few of his plays. He builds up the effect of complexity and subtlety by suggesting a number of levels of meaning. Thus, the inherited park symbolizes loneliness; the bench in The Zoo Story symbolizes both Peter's desire for autonomy and the inability to throw away the crutch he clings on for support. The fight that he puts up for the possession of his bench shows how strongly he identifies himself with it and can turn aggressive, even violent in order to retain it. The bench is like the solitary silent companion in whose presence Peter finds some unspoken, unworded solace. The glasses that Peter wears to read, symbolizes his moral blindness and guilt. Though he is blind to the real world, yet he is a spectator of life in general and of his own life in particular. He prefers to remain detached observer. The glasses help him stay behind them, thus distancing him from society. His glasses also imply his search for something beyond the realm of the physical. His myopic vision needs the support of glasses to enable him to reach at the truth of his existence. The book that he uses is a means of escape from reality. It also justifies the staying off his duties as a husband and father. The symbol of the book the George presented in Who's Afraid of Virginia Woolf? is the recurring image with the same meaning as it was for Peter. George use of the book enforces the idea that he wishes to avoid any direct confrontation with reality. George avoids the truth of Martha's infidelity by adopting an unconcerned and nonchalant attitude by holding the book. The book then is the deliberately sought obstacle that can thwart any unpleasant contact with reality.

The context of the play The Sandbox symbolizes the sandbox both as the cradle and the coffin while the baby sounds coming from the old lady stand for birth and death. The figure of the child who is named as Young Man in this play is a symbolic one. His series of movements recall "the beating and the fluttering of wings" which suggests that this character is "the Angel of Death".

In Albee's plays, the symbol of the box has often been used. The empty boxes of Grandma in The American Dream and in The Sandbox, the box used in The Zoo Story, relate playwright with his craze for Boxes. His fondness for the box persists in his other plays also-Box and Quotations from Chairman Mao Tse-tung, which are significant plays. The play Box, opens and closes with the monologues of a woman's voice which remains invisible or who is kept invisible. Most of these boxes are empty related with the emptiness of human existence. And in The American Dream the disappearance of the box is symbolic of the disappearance of the Grandma herself. In The Sandbox says Ruby Cohn:

> The child's play area is equated with Grandma's coffin and The American Dream, where Grandma with empty boxes is prophetic of her disappearance. In Box, the monstrous empty box evokes a coffin, not at once perhaps, but as we gradually absorb the words of the invisible woman's voice.[5]

A frequent use of religious symbols and allusion to Biblical figures and mythological symbols can be seen in Albee's works-The Zoo Story, Who's Afraid of Virginia Woolf? and in

The Play About the Baby. The dog-"a black monster of a beast; an over sized head, tiny ears and eyes ... (P. 170) in The Zoo Story, reminds Cerberus, the four headed monster who guards Hell. Black symbolizes darkness, death and the garb of the evil. Rose Zimbardo identifies the woman and dog as Milton's "sin and death"[6] Jerry, a thirty year old outcast is identified with Christ, and his descent into rooming house is comparable to God's descent into Hell. C.W.E. Bigsby remarks that Christian overtones are clear in The Zoo Story. He says "like Christ, Jerry is clearly designed to recall his message of love to be finally reinforced through his own sacrifice".[7] When Jerry dies he wipes the knife clear of finger prints, so as to absolve Peter, as Christ has absolved all those people who were responsible for his killings particularly. Peter has denied him thrice, but Jerry offers a triple affirmation, "Oh! My God, My God, My God!"

It is said that Who's Afraid of Virginia Woolf? also deals with some of the religious symbols. One possible interpretation forwarded by Benjamin Fulghum, Chairman of the English Department at Central Connecticut State College, is that George and Martha adopting the fantasy child is said to be a symbolic Christ child. George personifies the Protestant church and Martha, the Catholic making their family quarrel allegorical. Albee has himself said "I begin to suspect that I put an awful lot more Christian symbolism into my plays than I was consciously aware of."[8] In his later play Tiny Alice, the immoral life and corrupt practices prevailing in the church are exposed in the play. In The Play About the Baby, the Girl and the Boy appear like Adam and Eve in early days of Garden of Eden.

Some of Albee's names of characters have symbolic significance. The name Charlie implies manliness, strength and vigor; Nancy suggests grace and mercy. The Young Man who is portrayed in The American Dream, The Sandbox and Three Tall Women represent the future generation. Grandma calls him the American Dream: the dream which looks attractive from exterior, which has hopes of millions of people pinned upon it, which holds many promises but in reality is hollow from with in, numb, incomplete and useless like the Young Man. He is the American Dream personified that does not have the capacity to satisfy anyone who comes into contact with him.

The roles of some characters also have some symbolic role. The Old Woman in Quotations from Chairman Mao Tse-tung, symbolizes the future. The other three characters Mao, Tse, Tung together symbolize time and each becomes the representative of one aspect of time. They also represent the internal and social aspect of reality of the contemporary society.

Albee's plays are linked by a basic theme of human relations within the family. Mommy and Daddy in The Sandbox and The American Dream, Agnes and Tobias in A Delicate Balance, Woman and Man with Girl and Boy in The Play About the Baby, Gertrude and Henden in Finding the Sun and Stevie and Martin in The Goat or Who is Sylvia? constitute basic constructs for Albee but in a ritualized transaction they symbolically stand for the characters of his adoptive parents.

There are few individual symbols also in Albee's plays. The plays of absurd are extremely symbolic and the setting of play Seascape verifies it. It is on a deserted sand dune in bright sun, which suggests the absence of life's end. Traditionally sand also, suggests life's journey. The bright sunlight is associated with rebirth. The seawaters in Seascape symbolize the continuity of life, life moves on as the waters of the sea keep running eternally. Charlie's dip into the waters to find peace is suggestive of his returning to his mother's womb. Water is associated with sustenance; with regeneration of life and Nancy's suggestions to Charlie to re-live his childhood experience of going under water in search of life is an evidence of the stagnation that they have reached in their lives. The lizards that come up from the sea are symbolical of the evolution of mankind from water animals. From pre-historic age, lizards symbolize the constant and unending process of evolution, fast accelerating towards the machine age, the age of supersonic sounds and incredible speed. In the process of showing these animals gradually turning into human beings, Albee condemns and absorbs a whole course of natural history within the play.

Edward Albee captures the contradiction of the modern society and by substituting symbols he expresses his frustration. Albee like O'Neill uses the dramatic symbols which are grounded in traditional Christian names as well as props of the Theatre of Absurd evoking ironic, anguished response. Albee employed symbolism as a substitute for language to communicate the absurdity of certain human situation. Zimbardo A Rose subscribes to the view point that symbolism and naturalism blended effectively in Albee's style. He states:

> Concern with idea, rather than character or plot is not new in American theatre, nor is the use of symbolism for the realization of idea. There is however, about American plays which employ symbolism ... from O'Neil to William ... a strong suggestion of the gimmick ... what marks The Zoo Story as a new development of our drama is the way in which Albee blends symbolism with naturalism and the theme.[9]

A character in a play grows out of a given situation, is revealed through the whole range of interactions with other characters and exists only by means of a process of vital interdependence with the drama's plot of the play, themes and structure. It is the character which furthers the action and plot of the play. Characters in Albee's plays can be categorized as non-realistic, types and complex. He produces non-realist characters also, at times giving the role of the protagonist.

Albee, in The Death of Bessie Smith creates a character, who never appears on stage but is a motivating force of the action. Bessie Smith's death exposes the evil of apartheid in America and is instrumental in bringing forward the true nature of each character in the play. The theme of the play revolves around this character. In this play the story line develops only after Bessie Smith dies. In Who's Afraid of Virginia Woolf? the character Virginia Woolf doesn't appear on the stage at all till the end of the play.

In All Over, the same can be said of the dying man. The protagonist is the non-present character but never for a minute even, is he out of the minds of the characters on the stage. The audience is also constantly made aware of his presence. The play is centered on this dying and the conversation of the characters assembled to wait for his death revolves around him and it is through their dialogue that the dying man's character is revealed.

Albee moves a step further in his character portrayal in Box and Quotations, where characters literally are vanished in the physical sense. In Box for instance a physical flesh and blood character is replaced by a disembodied voice. Only the voice, which expresses Albee's ideas on art and culture, is heard. Character here becomes an abstraction, a vehicle for the expression of the dramatist's views on life.

In The Lady from Dubuque, the element which Albee describes as 'hallucinatory' revolve around the mother figure, who is again absent in the first part of the play is played by Elizabeth in the second act. In Three Tall Women, though the play begins with a meeting between elderly women in her nineties known as *A,* she becomes a non-character in Act II. It is only her image which is seen till the end of the play. Thus, though all these characters in the plays never appear on the stage directly or partly, they are the driving force behind other characters.

Edward Albee's plays present a specific world of ironic domesticity through the character of the child which ranges from that of the adopted infant, real or imagined baby, young man, dead child, imaginary person to that of grown-up homosexual son. According the Anne Paolucci, "Albee is a playwright who builds his characters from his own character".[10]

The absent child characters are familiar in Albee's plays as we see Teddy in A Delicate Balance, the illusory child in Who's Afraid of Virginia Woolf? Baby in The Play About the Baby. The stage convention by which a wadded-up blanket, represents a baby becomes a set up, and the young couple Boy and Girl concedes, grudgingly, that it has no baby-except that they can still hear it crying, though we can't, as the lights fade. The character of the Young Man appears in Three Tall Women, The American Dream and in The Sandbox. He is the recurring character in varied forms: Teddy in A Delicate Balance, Fergus in Finding the Sun, or YAM (Young American Playwright Vs Famous American Playwright) in FAM and YAM. In Who's Afraid of Virginia Woolf? the Young Man is the enigmatic, fictional son of Martha and George.

Albee gives functional names to his characters depersonalizing them totally. He never creates illusion that will involve us in the actions of the characters. Mommy, Daddy, Young Man, Intern, Nurse, Orderly, Boy, Girl, Best Friend, Cardinal, Lawyer, Butler, He, She, ... and the list is endless. All these characters are named after the functions. Albee does not consider these characters important enough to give them proper names for they lack individuality. They are just functionaries performing the given role in the society. They are identified in The American Dream, The Sandbox, Counting the Ways, Tiny Alice, The Death of Bessie Smith, The Play About the Baby and in few other plays.

It is also interesting to note that Albee always takes special interest in the choice of the names of his characters. George and Martha in Who's Afraid of Virginia Woolf? named after George and Martha Washington are significant in the historical patterns of the play. So are Peter and Jerry whose religious overtones are presented in The Zoo Story. In Tiny Alice, Alice is Albee's name for 'God's Head'.[11]

Albee continues to play with the names of characters in Finding the Sun and Three Tall Women, making equations. In

Finding the Sun, he presents equations and triangles to understand the complexity of life (A+B, C+D and B+D) and all the characters are named alphabetically from A to E. In Three Tall Women the equation is A=B=C, where *A* is an old woman around ninety three, *B* would look rather as *A* would have been at 52 and *C* looks rather as *t* would have at 26, they are interchangeable. They are separate women within the limits imposed by time and space but interfused beyond play. The characters in Fragments are divided into two sets: men and women aged between 20 and 65 and number one to four in ascending order. Each of the characters reads from a book of proverbs, making his characters play games through these, to show how the game of life is played.

Albee's women characters, especially in the early plays are more forceful, dominating and strong than their male counterparts. They are viragos, harridans, self-opinioned and independent. This may be partly attributed to Albee's personal life. In The Zoo Story, although no female characters are shown still they have some influence over their spouse. It is Peter's wife who decides not to have more children and compels Peter to comply with her wishes.

With the creation of the Nurse in The Death of Bessie Smith, Albee brings in American Drama a series of 'mommy portraits'. She is the first of the many portrayals to follow. In the Nurse character, Albee tries to present before us a woman trapped with in her prejudices, her false values and a woman who has never been able to think for herself. Albee creates a caricature of the modern American wife in Mommy of The Sandbox and The American Dream. The characteristics of all these women put together find expression in Martha's character.

There are samples of Albee's softened attitude towards women detected in the plays following Who's Afraid of Virginia Woolf? In Tiny Alice, Miss Alice serves only for the cause of Julian without any personal benefit. In A Delicate Balance,

Agnes, is the only woman who can retain the balance of the family. Nancy in Seascape, the Women in Listening, She in Counting the Ways as well as Stevie in The Goat or Who Is Sylivia are all women who never use foul or obscene language as the Nurse or Martha, but with their love manage to control the reins of their family. Thus in the later plays both the male and the female characters are of equal importance and none is given more footage than the other. The male characters are not as whimpering and passive as in the earlier plays.

Albee being an experimenter includes animals from dogs, cats and parakeets in The Zoo Story, the little 'zoo' as Jerry mockingly describes them to the goat in The Goat or Who is Sylvia? Ever since The Zoo Story, Albee's characters have engaged in bizarrely complex love affairs with animals, Jerry in The Zoo Story finds the love of his life in a stray dog. And Tobias in A Delicate Balance winds up his love by putting his cat to death and Albee in his recent play has shown the same love with a goat by a 50 year old Martin in The Goat or Who is Sylvia? Albee also introduces the talking lizards in the Seascape who come on to land to join a human couple. Like Jerry in The Zoo Story, Albee seems to be inspired by the desire 'to find out' more about the way people exist with animals, and the way animals exist with each other and with people too.

It is widely accepted that Thespis was the first dramatist in the conventional sense for it was he who introduced the concept of an actor/character in Greek drama. And through this, it is believed, he was able to achieve by segregating one member from rest of the chorus, thereby instituting the possibility of 'dialogue' in drama, and the beginning of dialogue was the real starting point of drama as it truly made it into an inter-active, inter-subjective and a living art form, distinct from poetry, dance or music. The purpose of a good dialogue is to reveal character. If the charm, the grace, the wit, the irony of the dialogue does not come from the character speaking, that dialogue fails.

Albee has proved himself to be a master of dialogue. He has, in fact, revolutionized the language of the American stage, extending verbal metaphor into visual settings of his plays, working isolated ironic reverberations, and using epic topography to maintain allegorical simplicity. Albee "has elaborated conversation with a sensitive ear to its complex musical effects, moving easily from major to minor mood, matching harmonic shifts with subtle tone changes from largo maestoso to pianissimo, heightening meaning with sudden reversals in style, juxtaposing cliché with pompous rhetoric, slang with archaic formality, hysterical fluency with monosyllabic exhaustion, establishing a variety of rhythms which are a constant surprise within the simple framework of the action."[12]

The basic tenets of the theatre of absurd proclaim the devaluation of language. The images of a stranger unable to communicate with those around him depicts the pointlessness, meaninglessness and ridiculous aspect of human condition. For Albee, language is a means by which one may go to "great lengths to avoid communication. Talk in order not to have to listen."[13] Since most of his plays deal with the lack of communication amongst the characters, language aids are more articulate and more cerebral, and there is more of talk than action in his plays. The result of this is that his language and his theatre appear exceedingly calculated and, to many even cold. Albee was aware of these problems himself and wondered: "What bothers people is the way my characters talk. They tend to be articulate. I don't understand why some think my plays are cold and intellectual."[14]

Language in Albee's plays has a similarity with the language of absurdists. In the drama of the absurd, language is gibberish, non sensical and impedes rather than furthers the purpose of communication. The failure of language is an important and major feature of the Theatre of the Absurd. The Sandbox and The American Dream are the best illustrations of this kind of language. They are full of meaningless words, repetitions for comic effects, cliché refrains. This kind of language prevents people from establishing a rapport or contact with one another. In The Zoo Story also Jerry desperately tries to communicate with Peter verbally but ultimately has to resort to physical violence in order to accomplish his aim.

Many of his characters are large as a mask to cover up their feelings; The American Dream is to a large extent about the increasing breakdown of communication. People neither listen nor pay attention, that's why Mommy says to Mrs. Barker, "won't you take off your dress?" instead of "won't you take of your coat?" (p. 37) The absurdity of the situation and the characters behavior is evident. Listening is based on the theme of not listening or paying attention to develop further communication. The Girl keeps complaining to the woman, "You don't listen! Pay attention, rather" (p. 73) The excitement and beauty of Albee's play lies in the way he digs into the unquestioned relationship which make a life, and realigns his characters, not in terms of what or who they are assumed to be but in terms of what they do. Those who have a clear identity have a less clear purpose and role in life. So the question, 'Who am I?' 'Who are you?' This precariousness of identity is underlined by one of the basic techniques Albee adopts in drawing attention to the theatre medium. While he develops a more or less uninterrupted stream of actions on the stage, he withdraws performers to make a direct address to the audience which is seen in Quotations from Chairman Mao, Tse-tung, The Man Who Had Three Arms, and Listening. The characterization of a role is further developed through this device. The actor or actress invites a judgment or shares a point of view with the audience.

Words are employed by Albee's characters as a means to get even with the other person, and also act as weapons to wound and hurt. Words are most important in Albee's plays. The most real thing about Jerry or Grandma or Martha is their words. Words unable to "relate", Albee's protagonists "look to language to forge whatever identity and relationship their lives have lacked."[15] Words provide these characters with the strength and confidence that their daily human contacts deny or inadequately furnish. It is through words that George takes revenge on Martha by playing "Get the Guests" and "Bringing up Baby". The wisest statement that he makes in the entire plays is when he tells Honey, "we all peel labels sweetie ... when you get down to bone ... and that's what gotta get at (pp. 124-125) Twice Martha summarizes: "George and Martha Sad, Sad, Sad," (p. 113) but George and Martha speak the wittiest lines of American Dream, "economical, euphonic and perfectly timed for our gaiety rather than sadness." (p. 113)

Edward Albee insists on the need to face reality. His characters make use of language to unmask reality but reality does not reveal itself wholly through language. Language is employed in Albee's characters to hide as well as reveal the truth. Albee considers language to be "both the disguise and the nakedness" and because these characters:

> tend to be far more articulate than a lot of peoples' character, that is their problem, I suppose, and therefore they more skillfully disguise it with language.[16]

No other American playwright has been so conscious of the power of language and so obsessed by it's precision as Albee. Taking this he said

> I suspect that my fascination with language to the extent it exists must stem from by first reading of Beckett. Nobody in the Twentieth Century theatre has been more precise in the use of language, more careful and more telling in the splitting of infinities.[17]

The plays of the absurd do not allow dialogue in the Shakespearean sense. An absurd play relies not on witty repartee or pointed dialogue; it rather consists of incoherent babblings. Albee's significant contribution to the drama of absurd lies in his rich language. Samuels also agrees regarding his use of language regard Who's Afraid of Virginia Woolf?

> Who's Afraid of Virginia Woolf? is successful because it uses the rich resources of Edward Albee's language both to peel back the veil on the unacknowledged terrors of 'normal' life and by denying their power to indulge its audiences sadism and flatter their ignorant hope. It removes the viewer from the action far enough to project his sense of life, but keeps him close enough to indulge his taste of blood.[18]

Albee's dialogues, simple yet effective, convey the themes of the play. The dialogues become instrumental in revealing inter-relationships of characters and setting the tone of the play. Not only is a dialogue necessary source of communication it also serves as a means of conveying the depth of complexity of character. In The Zoo Story, the course of the dialogue is rather arbitrary, sometimes disjointed, but nevertheless revealing Jerry's announcement of his visit to the zoo which begins in a low pitch but gradually reaches a high volume. Peter could hardly be affected by the loud declaration of Jerry that he has been to the zoo. The exchange of dialogues between the two clearly reflects the naturality of both the characters. The most striking feature is that each of them, particularly Jerry, conveys more monologues than dialogue. There is no reciprocity of statements or comments; there is no involvement which heightens the character of Peter. The short, crisp dialogues of the opening scenes become complicated and lengthier as the play progresses.

The dialogues of Who's Afraid of Virginia Woolf? are vulgar, sarcastic and bitchy. Almost every sentence spoken by George and Martha is like flinging stones at each other. Treating him almost as a mongrel dog, she mainly declares that she has "got tired of whipping", (P. 92) and calling him a "bastard"(P. 41) settles the score of his doubtful parentage, making him illegitimate product. Words like "Braying", "Cock-spaniel", "Hyena", "Satanic-Bitch", "monster", "a spoiled self-indulgent, willful, dirty-minded, liquor-ridden ..." (p. 94) for Martha and a "simp", a "blank", a "cipher", a "sour-puss", "muck-mouth", "paunchy", "bastard", "swampy", "floozie", and "son-of-a-bitch" for George are used quite often. Through these dialogues Albee reflects the degeneration of language in modern American people. Obsessed with violence and sex they talk in the same stagnating language which has no meaning, no depth, and no refinement of thought.

Tiny Alice begins with vulgar biting exchanges between Lawyer and the Cardinal which brings out the hatred the two characters have for each other. The use of the vernacular is like the release of the suppressed hatred each has for the other. The early vulgarism gives them an opportunity for raking memories of the past when they were school buddies. Their long standing enmity originated during the childhood period, and is carried into their adult year. The names they call each other are used again but with greater sadistic pleasure. The Lawyer calls the Cardinal a "swine" (P. 12) an "overstuffed, arrogant, pompous son of a profiteers and a whore" (P. 9) and for Cardinal "to devour its dead, scavenged prey, it would often chew into it ..."

The dialogues are mainly an outlet for hurling abuses at each other. The dialogues are vicious, animalistic and opprobrious. Dressed like gentlemen they show the offensive crude and deposed nature that they essentially possess. Violence, vulgarity, obscenity, bitterness, sharpness and bitchiness characterize Albee's dialogues in the earlier plays. In The American Dream, Mommy says:

> We are very poor! But then I married you, Daddy, and now we're very rich, I have a right to live off you because I married you, and because I used to let you on top of me and bump your uglies in. (P. 23)

Through these dialogues Albee reflects the degeneration of language in modern American people. Obsessed with violence and sex they talk in the same stagnating language which has no meaning, no depth and no refinement of thought. Martin Esslin pointing out Albee's play The American Dream says "The language of The American Dream resembles that of Ionesco in its masterly combination of clichés. But these clichés in their euphemistic, baby talk tone, are characteristically American."[19]

Albee's sharp dialogues can be seen in The Lady from Dubuque. The satire and the sting in them cannot be missed. Fred's cutting remark on Sam's and Jo's hospitality: "Where else can you come in this cold world, week after week, as regular as patch work, and he guaranteed ridicule and contempt?" (P. 30) illustrates this full. Albee, through his dialogues depicts the strained human relationship in contemporary American society. In the Marriage Play Gillian at one point exclaims at the hopelessness of the situation, "Oh! What a wrangled web we weave." (P.31)Each of the characters seems to be screaming like the Nurse in The Death of Bessie Smith, "I WANT OUT", without being able to find an opening to escape.

Some years later Albee's penchant for such sharp language dies down considerably and the dialogues display a more sober tone. The sentences, from the long drawn offensive verbal missiles of the earlier plays, are reduced to one line mostly, becoming abrupt and lacking continuity, the utterances are static and hardly illumine the character or move the play forward. Counting the Ways is one such play where the dialogue takes place between *He* and *She* suggesting total anonymity of character. Albee shows the very puniness of these characters who, quite unsure of each other, pretend and justify that love exists between them. The short and monosyllabic question and answer pattern of conversation shows insecurity and lack of warmth, that one holds towards the other. The method of dialogue delivery draws out the vast difference between the intention of the speaker and the ensuing result.

If one has to sum up Albee's contribution to the American stage, the immediate answer would surely be his language and dialogues. The language that he uses in his plays is something that arrests the attention of the people. As Bigsby says "Words are used to sustain illusion; laughter, to distract and to wound. ... Albee has brought to theatre not merely a magnificent command of language, a control of rhythm and tone which has never been rivaled in America, but also a sensitivity to dramatic tradition and particularly to the achievements of European dramatists, which gives his work a dimension all too often lacking in American writer."[20]

REFERENCES

1. Maurice Valency, *On the Theatre of No Meaning*, Playwrights, Lyricists, Composers on Theatre, ed., Otis L.Guernsey Jr. (1964, opt, New York: Dood, Mead and Company, 1974), p. 291.
2. *Writers at Work*; The Paris Review Interviews, Third Seriers, (New York: The Viking Press), p. 333.
3. Tennessee Williams –as qtd. In Prof. G.M.Sundaravalli, *Plastic Theatre–The evolution of Symbolism in the Plays of Tennessee Williams.*
4. Charles Chadwick, *Symbolism* (London: Metheun & Co Ltd., 1971), pp. 2-3.
5. Ruby Cohn, *Modern Drama*, Vol. 14; No. 2 (Sep. 1971), pp. 137-143.
6. Rose Zimbardo, *Symbolism and Naturalism in Edward Albee's The Zoo Story*, A Collection of Critical Essays ed., C.W.E.Bigsby, p. 23.
7. C.W.E. Bigsby, *A Critical Introduction to the Twentieth Century American Drama*, N.J. Prentice Hall.
8. Michael E.Rutenberg, *Interview with Edward Albee;* March 17, 1965.
9. Zimbardo A.Rose, *Symbolism and Naturalism in Edward Albee's The Zoo Story in Edward Albee*, ed., C.W.E. Bigsby, N.J.Prenice Hall 1975) p. 45.
10. Anne Paolucci, *From Tension to Tonic: The Plays of Edward Albee*, Carbondale: Southern Illionis, UP, 1971.
11. Richard M.Coe, *Beyond Absurdity: Albee's Awareness of Audience in Tiny Alice*, Modern Drama XVIII, 4th December 1975.
12. Anne Paolucci, *From Tension to Tonic: The Plays of Edward Albee*, Carbondale: Southern Illionis, UP, 1971.

13. Krohn and Wasserman, *An Interview with Edward Albee*, (March 18, 1981), p. 19.
14. *Ibid*, p. 20.
15. New York Times, May 23, 1978 Internet.
16. Arthur K.Oberg, *Edward Albee: His Language and Imagination*, Prairier Schioner, No. 40, 1966, p. 143.
17. Ruby Cohn, *The Verbal Murders of Edward Albee*, Minneapolis: University of Minnesota Press, 1969, p. 143.
18. *Ibid*. p. 143.
19. Martin Esslin, *The Theatre of the Absurd*, New York: Double Day, 1961.
20. C.W.E. Bigsby (ed) *Edward Albee: Twentieth Century Views* (Englewood Cliffs, N.J: Prentice Hall, 1975.

7
Summing Up
All Over

The HEALTH of a nation, a society can be determined by the art it demands.[1]

Albee 'is the product of his culture'. He reflects every strength and weakness of the culture, both as an artist and as a human being. It would be no exaggeration to say that Albee has emerged as America's 'first dogged culture watchdog'. The proof of this fact is that of his steady and valid presence on the stage for four decades till now, ever since he wrote and produced The Zoo Story, (1958). Thrice winner of the Pulitzer prize, the first time in 1967 for A Delicate Balance, Seascape in 1975, Three Tall Women 1994, it looks as though the best is yet to come from this seventy plus year old playwright whose avowed mission in life is to make the American part of the universe sit up and take notice of its illnesses through the transforming power of art. Art is not a mere escape or entertainment, which it had been in America till the early 20th century. Albee frequently uses his lecturers to describe how he believes the art can be a catalyst for change. He says "The job of the arts, is to hold a mirror up to us and say: "Look, this is how you really are. If you don't like it, change."[2]

Albee belongs to the charmed circle of a few sensitive and cultivated minority called philosophers who are gifted with an awareness of the meaning of the problems afflicting society, for as Tonlin would put it, "The philosopher is one who abstracts the real issue from the tangle of emotions that cling round it."[3] Historical, philosophical and dramatic unity of vision is seen in nearly 25 plays of Edward Albee from The Zoo Story to his last one.

Edward Albee was the first dramatic satirist in his generation who vociferously attacked American self-complacency that had become an integral part of the American social structure. The age that is represented in his plays is conspicuous by its moral depravity, emotional and cultural sterility, and intellectual void and spiritual nullity. All the institutions of society-social, political and religious, as recognized by Albee, have collapsed; the ethics, politics and private life of man have proved to be corrupt and bereft of meaning. Albee's plays show "what a sad and shabby time we live in."[4] The world according to him is threatened by moral vacuity and intellectual stupidity; civilization having lost its goal is at its ebb tide.

Edward Albee is not merely a social critic, but he is rather 'a demonic social critic' as he describes himself. He is truthfully bitter in his attack of a social system which fails in its duty of creating responsible citizens. He presents characters which must strip themselves of all pretence if they want to survive as respectable individuals and accept their duty towards others. The effect he seeks in this role is to make man review his present state and struggle to amend it. In The American Dream and The Death of Bessie Smith, and The Play About the Baby, the characters are vain, vacuous and false. Cruelty and violence dominates their lives. The portrayals of Mommy, Mrs. Barker and the Nurse, and the Boy and Girl reveal the horror of life that Albee reiterates in his plays. These characters are representatives of a society that has lost its moral and social values and is fast moving towards inevitable destruction.

Albee is a progressive writer whose criticism of society is not just meant to reveal a die hard attitude but also to encourage and recognize change or improvement as his later plays suggest. The metamorphosis of Albee's mind is in direct relation to his plays. There is a transition to be seen in Albee, from intense bitterness and satire to a mellowed acceptance of society at large. He has been able to rise from personal to impersonal, from a subjective involvement to an objective detachment with his characters.

Exploration of the human mind rather than the portrayal of the superficial layers of humanity have been the central issue in many of Albee's plays. The search for identity is a recurrent theme in most of his plays as we find in The Zoo Story, Tiny Alice, All Over, The Lady from Dubuque, Finding the Sun, and other plays of Albee. The search is carried out through family relationships which concern both real and imagined parents and children, and weighed by the impact of death on survivors. Since time weighs heavy on man and "THE WHOLE WORLD IS FLYING APART!!" Albee feels that the search for the self creates an awareness of the realities of existence and enables man to seek a meaning in life.

Edward Albee's primary target is the foundation of the family, its matriarchal structure, the waning away of the older generation and the emasculation of the third generation. The reason for dying middle class life and the disharmony in families have been traced back by Albee to the disturbing social condition prevailing in their time. The family unit, for him is a symbolic microcosm of society which yearns for security, understanding, communication and love. Albee's families are stripped off essential unifying bonds. For his characters the emotion of love and kindness are not the basis of any relationship. The institution of marriage, more than anything else is a farce, in which there never exists any lasting bond based on faith and affection.

By placing American middle class family at the heart of his works, Albee has created a picture of the American society and the American way of life. The playgoers of his generation have been called on to "sit and watch ... (to) have so clear a picture, see everybody moving through his own jungle ... an insight into all the reasons, all the needs."[5] Although some of the Albee's plays present bachelors like Jerry, Jack, Julian and others and celebrate celibacy, his concern has been family unit; he once stated, "I've nothing against marriage. I think it's a perfectly possible way to love."[6]

The family which is the source of safety and security has been the source of struggles and psychological tensions. In the American society the family itself is in a 'delicate balance'. Although the fundamental lack of love and stress on wealth and status, conflicts of temperaments and infidelity of the spouse have posed a threat to the family structure, the family unit has been usually preserved. Emphasis has been laid on the ideals of the family life. Albee tries to restore the affection between husband and wife, parents and children and speak for the family solidarity; they are keen to prevent family disruption. Individuals' over estimation of false social values which caused emotional, economical and sexual friction in them affected their family and marital life. Many families, on the verge of disintegration are due to the husbands desire for romantic interludes even after middle age, reflecting the current permissiveness of the society. Sex has been a problem in families, as one finds in The American Dream, Who's Afraid of Virginia Woolf?, A Delicate Balance, The Goat or Who is Sylivia?

Albee has identified the failure of contemporary Americans in their family life to be the cause of the failure of the American society, culture and in general the decline of the Western Civilization. Albee does not mean to criticize the family and marriage as such, but his dispute against the American family, becomes a commentary on all human relationships. He demonstrates through this bizarre drama The American Dream the danger of accepting too readily the values that society puts on people in the family and marriage as well as in the name of class, race, religion and politics that are well substantiated in Tiny Alice and The Death of Bessie Smith. Peter Wolfe states, "By dwelling into the tightly knit family group (or the group that recognizes itself as a family), Albee enables himself to dramatize in greater depth a social organism which is disoriented at its source"[7]

Deeply outraged by his personal experiences of unhappiness, disillusionment and disappointment, Albee makes the American society of his creative world suffer the same sense of helplessness, impotency, callousness and indifference. However, with time, the seething anger and volatile hatred of a matriarchal society was replaced by a mellowed acceptance of the family as an important unit of society. His attitude towards family became more favorable and as such his later plays directly reveal an improvement in the delineation of family. Members are no longer critical of each other, or apathetic towards others feelings but make efforts to bring harmony and cordiality in their relations. The earlier mother and father figures developed from destructive agents to mature character capable of making their own decisions. The non-living and inhuman Mommy of The American Dream turns into the love-dominated wife-mistress of All Over. This is a dramatic evidence of Albee's shift in views. The dull submissive Daddy figure of the early plays contrasts sharply with the authority figure of Tobias in A Delicate Balance. Tobias' miraculous change can be seen from his non-involvement in family affairs to a decision taking father and husband.

Albee has exploded the illusion of American civilization. He has captured in modern terms the dramatic power of man, man destroyed by his own acts still clinging to life, still in search of meaning. In The Lady from Dubuque, Albee has depicted the fateful struggle in man shattering realities of life in solving the basic problems of existence. Albee calls attention to the fact that unless a man is dead to an unreal life he can never be awakened to a new, real life.

Albee's keen interest in the psychological, social and physical aspects of man led him to observe his condition in both states - life and death. As a result of being under illusion, the lives of Albee's protagonists are spiritually barren. It is not that they are confronted with physical death. Albee asserts that the nature of death and illusion are inseparable. Generally, Albee's characters seek to escape their death in life situation by destroying the very illusions they have imprisoned themselves in. Jerry, the Nurse, Martha and many other protagonists are all victims of their illusions. They strive to come out of their cramped, warped environment by breaking those barriers which obstruct their confrontation with reality. For Albee, their illusion is a mask which separates man from man and from truth which ends in death to a certain extent of the potential creativity of the individual. Preferring the end of life rather the living state of death or the spiritually withered life, Albee's characters find solace and peace in physical death. From The Zoo Story to Tiny Alice death becomes a means by which Albee's characters free themselves from their illusions willfully, they show courage and hope for better times like George in Who's Afraid of Virginia Woolf?

The world which Albee observes is entropic. Its basic impulse is a disintegrative force. His subject is what Agnes, in A Delicate Balance, describes in a nutshell: "the gradual ... demise of intensity, the private preoccupations, the substitutions."[8] That is to say, he means alienation by the 'demise of intensity', institutionalization by 'private pre-occupations', illusion by 'substitution'. He takes into account the way in which relationships dissolve and how individuality collapses. Bigsby points out that Albee's concern is "to establish the connection between personal relations and public policy, as he is to balance what is given with what can still be changed."[9]

One observation about Albee is that he never completes his plays, that is, he ends the play abruptly giving room for ambiguous thoughts. The action never takes beyond perception, because Albee doesn't want to give his audience any comfort or reassurance, no desire to reinforce complacency. He presents his point of view and after having done it leaves the play with the audience so that the completion should be carried out by the audience in the line that Albee has already drawn out. He does not choose to dramatize the social and moral world which he has advocated, and therefore his plays remain open ended.

Albee's career as a writer has been accompanied by an increasing concern with the practical medium of theatre. From the outset he championed theatre in America and has actively promoted new works, both his own and that of other, predominantly younger dramatists. In more recent years he has become active as the director of his own plays. In 1963 he felt that the ideal performance was the one he had experienced in his own imagination: "There is only one true, correct, hard, ideal performance of a play, and that is mine, and I saw it when I was writing".[10] By 1978, when he was engaged in a tour of five of his early plays, he was no longer prepared to leave the 'ideal performance' as the property of the writer, and evidently felt dissatisfied with the sort of directions to be seen in the theatre: "I think I can get clarity and precision, by directing myself. The direction may not be flashy but I'm not really interested in flash".[11] The qualities which Albee speaks of complement is his articulate style of writing.

Edward Albee's greatest achievement and contribution to American drama is his powerful language and the weaving of musical form and dramatic structure. He revolutionized the language of the American stage with his repartee, monologues and dialogues. Box and Quotations and Who's Afraid of Virginia Woolf? exemplify his skill in creating musical dramatic structure. He has assimilated and used innovatively all the known dramatic techniques from realism to meta theatre and has preserved for posterity, a unique dramatic record of American theatre. The younger playwrights are influenced by him in his mode of writing. The works of Sam Shepard and David Mamet are very much similar to Albee's plays. Music plays an important role in his plays for he feels that it is only through music emotions can be communicated.

Albee can be classified with theatrical experimenters whose work jumped the boundaries of American Drama. Beginning with the reviews of Albee's earliest works, Albee's has gathered a wide variety of critical opinion, many commentators note Albee's inventiveness and insight into society and human nature while at the same time responding negatively to the tone or structure of his dramas. For example, although The American Dream was faulted by some as defeatist and nihilistic, it was also praised for its savage parody of traditional American values. Albee commented: "Is the play offensive? I certainly hope so; it was my intention to offend-as well as amuse and entertain."[12] While several of Albee's plays written since 1962 have failed commercially and elicited stinging reviews for their abstract classicism and dialogue, many scholars have commended Albee's commitment to theatrical experimentation and refusal to indulge to commercial pressure. His failures at the box-office can be well known as his critical successes. "His plays tend to be dark and challenging; the themes of solitude, loss and death recur throughout his works."[13]

Like Ibsen and Strindberg, Albee has identified only sickness and loneliness in existence. Unlike nihilist who believes that life is nothing, Albee values life and its standards he tries to find meaning in life by focusing attention on the human condition in the modern world. Albee has been given admission to the group of absurdists by eager critics like Esslin, for his first two one act plays, The Zoo Story and The American Dream are concerned with the problems of alienation and search for self. Albee believes that man must find meaning in his absurd existence, as Jerry endeavor even at the cost of his life. The playwrights like Beckett, Ionesco, Pinter and Adamov are satisfied with exposing the absurd lives lived by men, unaware and unconscious of the reality. But, Albee is convinced that the individuals' absurdity is their own making. "We manufacture such a portion of our own despair."[14] and he re-affirms his belief that change is possible if the human situations are confronted. By leaving some space in the Box, he suggests that still there is hope for orderliness and harmony in the world. His most optimistic play Seascape ends with an invitation to his contemporaries to begin the march towards the change.

With all his success, Albee might easily be expected to retire, but his indefatigable nature and interest in social issues continues to motivate him to create higher art. Despite having been explored extensively, Albee's mysterious mind still leaves some untrodden and unknown areas to be discovered. Albee's work consistently demonstrates a commitment to these ideals as he continues to challenge audiences intellectually and morally. He continues to create and work towards projects that give them better choice. He remains today one of America's most celebrated and influential playwrights and a true friend of the American theatre.

Albee has once remarked that "till the society changes, plays will be written criticizing the American way of life."[15] Perhaps we can best sum up Albee's reputation as a controversial playwright by noting more modestly that, although he has been "condemned by some and worshipped by others, Edward Albee is clearly the most compelling American playwright to explode upon the Broadway stage, since Tennessee Williams and Arthur Miller in mid-forties."[16]

REFERENCES

1. Edward Albee, *Which Theatre is the Absurd One?* New York Times Magazine (February 25, 1962), p. 64.
2. Internet Online *Award Winning Dramatist Edward Albee to Present Puget Sound Lecture*. January 10, 2006, p. 1.
3. Tonlin, E.W.F. *Philosophers of East and West: The Quests for the Meaning of Existence in Eastern and Western Thought* (London: Oak Tree Books Limited, 1986), p. 371.

4. Edward Albee, *All Over* Best American Plays, ed. Clive Barnes (New York: Crown Publishers, 1975), p. 152.
5. Edward Albee: *A Delicate Balance*, 1966, rpt, New York Athenueun, p. 128.
6. Albee, Interview in Bevverwyck Quoted in Wages Walter, ed. The Playwrights Speak (New York: Delacorte Press, 1967) p. 30.
7. Peter Wolfe, *The Social Theatre of Edward Albee*, p. 254.
8. Edward Albee; *A Delicate Balance*, (New York, 1967) p. 82.
9. C.W.E. Bigsby, *A Critical Introduction to the Twentieth Century American Drama*, N.J. Prentice Hall, 1975, p. 290.
10. Newsweek, 4 Feb., 1963.
11. San Francisco Chronicle, 12 Oct, 1978, Qtd. Gerry McCarthy, Edward Albee, Macmillan Publishers Ltd., 1987, p. 29.
12. Internet Online *Award Winning Dramatist Edward Albee to Present Puget Sound Lecture*. January 10, 2006. p. 1.
13. Ruby Cohn, *Modern Drama*, Vol. 14, p. 44.
14. Edward Albee, *A Delicate Balance*, (New York, 1967) p. 126.
15. Albee, Interview in Beverwyck Quoted in Wager Walter ed. The Playwrights Speak p. 48.
16. Anonymous, *Albee. Odd Man in on Broadway*, p. 49 qtd Richard E.Amacher, 'Edward Albee', Twayne Publishers, Inc. New York, 1969; p. 170.

Bibliography

PRIMARY SOURCES

(Arranged Chronologically)

The Zoo Story, The Death of Bessie Smith, The Sandbox. New York: Coward McCann, 1960.

The American Dream. New York: Coward McCann, 1961.

Who's Afraid of Virginia Woolf? New York: Atheneum, 1962; London: Jonathan Cape, 1964.

Tiny Alice. New York: Atheneum, 1966; London: Jonathan Cape, 1966.

A Delicate Balance. New York: Atheneum, 1966; London: Jonathan Cape, 1968.

Box and Quotations from Chairman Mao Tse-tung. New York: Atheneum, 1969; London: Jonathan Cape, 1970.

All Over. New York: Atheneum, 1971; London: Jonathan Cape, 1972.

Seascape. New York: Atheneum, 1975; London: Jonathan Cape, 1976.

Counting the Ways and Listening. New York: Atheneum, 1977.

The Lady from Dubuque. New York: Atheneum, 1980.

Finding the Sun. Antaeus 66 (1991) 15-43.

The Man who Had Three Arms. New York: Atheneum, 1987.

Marriage Play. Harmondsworth: Penguin, 1987.

Three Tall Women Harmondsworth: Penguin 1995.

The Play About the Baby New York: Dramatists Play Service, 2002.

The Goat or Who is Sylvia? New York: Dramatists Play Service, 2003.

SECONDARY SOURCES

Amacher, Richard E., *Edward Albee,* Twayne Publishers, New York, 1969.

Bigsby C.W.E., *Confrontation and Commitment,* Columbia, University of Missouri Press, 1968.

Bigsby, C.W.E., *A Critical Introduction to Twentieth Century American Drama,* Vol. III, Cambridge: Cambridge University Press, 1984.

Burgers, Earnest, W. & Lockee, Harvey, *The Family*, New York: American Book Co. 1945.

Camus, Albert, *The Myth of Sisphus,* tr. Justin O'Brien (London: Hamish Hamilton, 1960).

Cavan, Ruth Shonle, *The American Family,* 3rd ed. (1963, rpt, New York: Thomas Y Growell Company, 1966.

Choudari, A.D., *The Face of Illusion in American Drama,* Delhi: Macmillan Company, 1972.

Cohn, Ruby, *New American Dramatist,* London: Macmillan, 1982.

Cohn, Ruby. & Dukore, Benard. F., *Twentieth Century of the Cotemporary Theatre*, New York: Random House, 1966.

Coleridge, Samuel, *The Rime of Ancient Mariner,* Dr. Raghukul Tilalk, Rama Publications, 1977.

Debusscher, Gilbert, *Edward Albee: Tradition and Renewal,* Translated by Anne. D. Williams, Brussels: American Studies Centre, 1967.

Deshpande, L.S.I., *The Theatre of the Absurd in Marathi,* qtd Jean Paul Sartre 'Essays on Comparative Literature and Linguistic, New Delhi: Sterling Publishers, 1984.

Flannagan, William, *Edward Albee: An Interview in Writers at Work,* 3rd Series (New York: Viking Press, 1967).

Gassner, John, *Directions in Modern Theatre and Drama,* 1958, rpt New York, Crown Publishers Inc., 1970.

Jung, Carl Gustav, *The Undiscovered Self,* Trans R.F.C. Hall, New York, 1957.

Martin Esslin, *Introduction to Absurd Drama* Harmodsworth, Penguin Books Ltd., 1976.

Martin, Esslin, *The Theatre of the Absurd* Penguin Books, London, March, 1961.

McCarthy, Gerry, *Edward Albee,* Macmillan Publishers Ltd., 1987.

Paolucci, Anne, *From Tension to Tonic: The Plays of Edward Albee* Carbondale: Southern Illinois University Press, 1972.

Rao, Nageswar G., *Encounter with Nothing* Sri Venkatewara University Press, Tirupati, 1979.

Roudane, Mathew C., *Understanding Edward Albee,* Columbia: University of South Carolina Press, 1987.

Rutenberg, Michael E., *Edward Albee: Playwrights in Protest,* New York: Avon, 1969.

Singh, C.P., *Edward Albee: The Playwright of Quest,* Vittal Publication, Delhi, 1987.

Valency, Maurice, *On the Theatre of No Meaning,* Playwrights, Lyricists, Composers on Theatre, New York: Dood, Mead and Company, 1974.

Wasserman, Julian, *Edward Albee: An Interview and Essays,* Lee Lecture Series, University of St. Thomas, Houstan, 1983.

Yeats, W.B., *The Second Coming,* Selected Poems, London 1956.

ARTICLES

Ashmore, Jerry, *Interdisciplinary Roots of the Theatre of the Absurd,* Modern Drama, Vol. 14, No. 1; 1971.

Baldwind, James, *Theatre, The Negro in and Out of it,* New York, 1966.

Brown, Daniel, *Albee's Targets,* Satire News Letter (Spring, 1969).

Brustein, Robert, *Fragments from a Cultural Explosion,* New Republic, CXLIV, March 27, 1961.

Chadwick, Charles, *Symbolsim*, London: Metheun & Co. Ltd., 1971.

Clurman, Harold, *'Seascape'- Criticism* New York, Vol. 220 (March 13, 1975).

Coe, R.M., *Beyond Absurdity: Albee's Awareness of Audience in Tiny Alice*, Modern Drama, Vol. 18, December 1975.

Cohn, Ruby, *The Verbal Murders of Edward Albee,* Minneapolis: University of Minnesota Press, 1969.

Diehl, Digby, *Edward Albee Interviewed*; Transatlantic Review, No. 13 (Summer 1963).

Franzblan, Abraham.N., *A Psychiatrist Looks at Tiny Alice,* Saturday Review, XLVIII, 30, January 1965.

Gabbard, Luciana, P., *Edward Albee's 'Triptych on Abandonment'* Twentieth Century Literature, 28, (Spring 1983).

Gill, Brendin, *Box & Quotations From Chairman Mao Tse-tung,* New York, Vol. 44 (October, 12, 1969).

Howe, Irving, *A World More Attractive: A View of Modern Literature and Politics,* New York, 1965.

Kingsley, Lawrence, *Reality and Illusion: Continuity of a Theme in Albee*, Educational Theatre Journal, 25, (March 1973).

Kroll, Jack, *'Seascape'-Criticism,* New York, Vol. 85 (February 3, 1975).

Lewis, Allan, *Plays and Playwrights in the Contemporary Theatre*, New York: Crown Publishers, Inc, 1965.

Luere, Jeane, *A Review from Three Tall Women,* Theatre Journal, Vol. 44, No. 2 May 1922.

Lyons, Charles, *Two Projections of the Isolation of the Human: Brenchts I'm Dickicht Der and Albee's The Zoo Story,* Drama Survey IV (1965).

Mary, Nillan, A., *Albee's The Zoo Story: Alienated Man and Nature of Love,* Modern Drama XVI, June 1973.

Meserve, Walter, J., *An Outline History of American Drama*, New Jersey: Toronto, 1970.

Oberg, Arthur, *Edward Albee: His Language and Imagination,* Prairie Schooner, (Spring, 1966).

Samuels, Charles Thomas, *The Theatre of Edward Albee,* The Massachusetts Review, Vol. 6; No. 1 (Autumn-Winter 1964-65).

Slykes, Carole. A., *Albee's Beast Fables: The Zoo Story and A Delicate Balance*, Educational Theatre Journal, Vol. 25 (December 1973).

Tallmer, Jerry, *Edward Albee: Playwright*, New York Post, Sunday Magazine Section, November 4, 1962

Tonlin, E.W.F., *Philosophers of East and West: The Quests For the Meaning of Existence in Eastern and Western Thought,* London, 1986.

Trilling, Diana, *The Riddle of Albees: Who's Afraid of Virginia Woolf?* In A Collection of Critical Essays.

Withrington, Paul, *Language of Movement in Albee's 'The Death of Bessie Smith;* Twentieth Century Literature, 13; No. 2 (July 1867).

ON-LINE (INTERNET)

www.google search

The John F. Kennedy centre for the Performing Arts.

Bottoms, Stephen, Introduction. The Man who had three lines.

Anon, "Albee : Odd Man in on Broadway; News Week, Feb. 1963.

'Interlude', Chaote Literary Magazine.

A Playwright Speaks: An Interview with Edward Albee.

New York Times (18 April, 1971).

Harold Hobson, Christian Science Monitor (11 February 1972).

Tom Scanlar, "The Family World of American drama, Family, Drama and American Dreams", p. 193.

Edward Albee, Planned Wilderness: Interview, Essays and Bibliography ed. Patricia De La Fu ente (Edinburg, Texas. Pan American University, 1980).

News Week Feb. 11, 1980.

Interview on 22nd March 1965, at Billy Rose Theatre, New York.

News Week, Jan. 4th 1965.

Mel Gussow, A Singular Journey begins.

New York Times, May 23, 1978.

Award Winning Dramatist Edward Albee to Present Puget Sound Lecture, January 10, 2006.

Peter Wolfe, The Social Theatre of Edward Albee, New York, 1967.

News Week, 4th Feb. 1963.

Index